THE FIREFLY EFFECT

WHEN SYSTEMS BREAK, FIREFLIES RISE

THE FIREFLY EFFECT

HOW TO LEARN, LEAD, AND THRIVE IN THE AGE OF AI

RUSSELL JOHN CAILEY

FOREWORD BY TRUNG LE

The Firefly Effect: How to Learn, Lead, and Thrive in the Age of AI

Russell John Cailey

Published by Game Changer Publishing

Paperback ISBN: 978-1-968250-65-2
Hardcover ISBN: 978-1-968250-66-9
Digital ISBN: 978-1-968250-67-6

www.GameChangerPublishing.com

For Solmaz

And for my parents, John and Denise,
and my brother Neil

TABLE OF CONTENTS

"The future is already here—it's just not evenly distributed."

— William Gibson

FOREWORD

When Russell asked me to write this foreword, I had one question: "What's the title?" "The Firefly Effect," he said. I paused—then smiled. As a longtime student of living systems, he had me at emergence.

I once heard a biologist describe a summer night in the wetlands. At first, fireflies blink at random—scattered points of light. Then a pulse passes from one insect to the next. A few seconds later the meadow breathes in perfect rhythm, thousands of tiny bioluminescent lamps flashing as one. No conductor, no CEO, no queen. Just a pattern rising from countless simple signals. That is emergence: a spontaneous order that grows from simple actions, creating something more beautiful and unpredictable than any strategic plan could deliver.

The Firefly Effect: How to Learn, Lead, and Thrive in the Age of AI offers more than an account of our turbulent times. It draws us into its living environment, urging us to imagine new possibilities for how we learn, work, and live. Here, Russell challenges us to rethink what matters most in education and to design a learning ecology fit for our era. In an age increasingly dominated by artificial intelligence, living systems like fireflies remind us that emergence is both a seed of hope and a reminder of our collective responsibility.

Who is Russell inviting into the circle of futurists? It's the parents staring at each other at the kitchen table, wondering whether tomorrow's machines will eclipse a child's hard-earned grades or how they'll afford the endless rise in college costs. It's the professional whose expertise keeps shrinking each time a new AI model rolls out. It's the leader racing to rewrite strategy as the world outpaces the Monday morning operations meetings. And it's the educator standing alone in the classroom, asked to prepare young people for an unpredictable future.

These individuals feel isolated—like distant points of light—until someone shows them how their separate rhythms can synchronize into something larger.

Russell is that someone. A designer of learning, an intentional troublemaker, he spends his days asking what comes after the familiar curriculum and classroom. Decades of workshops, kitchen-table brainstorms, and global field projects have taught him one thing: The future favors the curious more than the prepared. He calls himself the stone in education's shoe, the necessary irritant that keeps us moving.

Discomfort, he reminds us, is a form of joyful suffering, the signal that an outdated system is ready to be replaced. When a structure no longer serves its purpose, new ideas gather at the edges, waiting to shine.

In Russell's lived experiences, curiosity behaves like a living organism. It grows when people exchange questions, test hunches, and share unfinished thoughts. Leadership, then, is less about directive and more about creating conditions: removing old rituals, asking deeper questions, making space for unlikely collaborations. Create the environment, and ideas will collide and multiply.

Why fireflies? Because they show how real change happens through attention, adaptation, and courageous response, not through control. You won't find a single "how-to" formula in these pages. AI is too new and wild, the world too fluid. What you will find are frameworks tempered in the chaos of fieldwork, sketches drawn over the ruins of standardized tests, and a quiet confidence that even a few determined people can make a meaningful dent in the status quo.

Read with an open mind. Pause when a story stirs you. Share the book with a colleague, a young person, a leader, and see how your separate questions might intersect, flash by flash, into something neither of you could have planned.

Let the emergence experiment begin.

Trung Lê
Director of Design
reGenerating Education

Trung Lê has dedicated his 35-year career to transforming educational environments. As founder of Third Teacher+, Wonder by Design, 180 Studio and Project: TEAM10, he leads practices dedicated to revolutionizing learning spaces through design. Lê has received awards from the Chicago, Illinois, and national chapters of the American Institute of Architects (AIA). His humanity-centered design approach has earned recognition from AIA, The Committee on Architecture for Education, Architectural Record, and Edutopia, while his collaboration on "The Third Teacher" project with Bruce Mau established him as a recognized voice in educational design. Lê has blogged for Fast Company, speaks at TEDx and other international forums on the intersection of learning, design, and architecture.

In 2024, Lê accepted an invitation to join a global coalition to build reGenerating Education, a strategy-design-build studio with a single focus: designing new regenerative ecosystems for living, working, and learning. This living laboratory builds on his extensive experience in independent and international school design, where his award-winning projects demonstrate the power of design to transform learning and teaching.

WHO THIS BOOK IS FOR

This isn't just an education book. It's not just a business book. It's a **human book** for everyone facing the reality that AI is reshaping how we learn, lead, and thrive.

If you're a parent, you're watching your child navigate a world where the skills you learned in school may be obsolete by the time they graduate. At the same time, the testing system that defines our success might be destroying their curiosity.

If you're a professional, you're wondering if your expertise will matter when AI can do your job faster. You're caught between learning new tools and preserving what makes you essential.

If you're a leader, you're trying to transform your organization and build a slower world while managing people who fear being replaced by machines.

If you're an educator, you're balancing pressure to prepare students for tests with the knowledge that real-world success requires skills that no test can measure.

No matter who you are, the firefly frameworks offered here will work for you because the core challenge is the same: How do we remain authentically human while thriving alongside artificial intelligence?

At its core, this book aims to help those about to potentially make their biggest mistake, which is waiting for an external light in this age of disruption instead of generating their own.

Your light matters, regardless of your role.

At the start of each chapter, you'll see a signal of the future. Treat these as diary entries from a possible future. The world is changing, and these signals serve as warnings to those failing to adapt.

Statistics and examples are current as of early 2025. In our rapidly changing world, some numbers may have shifted by publication, but the patterns and principles remain constant.

***Note**: A comprehensive glossary of firefly concepts and key terminology can be found at the end of this book for easy reference.*

INTRODUCTION

LIGHTING THE FIRST SPARK

"The only impossible journey is the one you never begin."

— Tony Robbins

Signal from the Future*: A young executive activates her digital twin to handle the morning's forty-seven emails, school calls, and overdue bills. Within minutes, everything's done—in her voice, her style, her decisions. Her biggest challenge today? Pretending she still needs eight hours to do three hours of real work.*

I want you to imagine something that might disturb you. Imagine waking up ten years from now to discover that a digital avatar, not a human being but artificial intelligence, has just won the Nobel Prize for Literature. Its novel, written in seventeen languages, simultaneously explores the deepest questions of human existence with a beauty and an insight that left critics speechless. Or, imagine discovering that your child's learning has been revolutionized, not by better teachers or smaller class sizes, but by bio-integrated devices that enhance their cognitive abilities in real time, personalizing every moment of their educational experience based on their unique neural patterns. Or perhaps more unsettling, imagine learning that while you slept last night, your digital twin—a perfect simulation of your thoughts, preferences, and decision-making patterns—has been living a parallel life online, maintaining your relationships, closing business deals, even making commitments you're now bound to honor. These aren't science-fiction scenarios; they're emerging realities that we need to prepare for today.

In the world of education, researchers are currently developing attention-tracking systems that can detect when students lose focus during digital learning sessions.[1] Meanwhile, AI scored in the 88th percentile on law school entrance exams[2] and the 93rd percentile on the SAT, and Google's quantum computer solved a complex problem in two hundred seconds that would take our most powerful supercomputers ten thousand years.[3] This is just the beginning.

But here's what should terrify you: While AI scored in the upper fifth percentile on the SAT, your child is still memorizing facts for tests from a system designed in the 1950s. We're training human brains to be inferior computers while machines learn to out-create us.

So, who am I, and why does all this "AI stuff" matter? I've spent two decades discovering what happens when learning breaks free from traditional constraints as part of a nomadic education experiment. While most educators work within existing systems, I've built learning communities that operate entirely outside them, where humans tackle real problems in real-world environments, where curiosity drives the curriculum, and where the world becomes the classroom.

This wasn't planned. It emerged from a simple question: *What if we stopped trying to prepare students in static classrooms and started helping them engage with the actual world around them?* That question launched a career: building learning ecosystems where breakthrough moments happen through direct experience rather than textbook theory.

These moments rocked me to my core, challenging everything I thought I knew about resilience, empathy, and human potential. The most profound learning came from the program participants in Kolkata as part of an educational collaboration. The organization's approach challenged everything I thought I knew about education and recovery. They built learning communities centered on trust, creative expression, and peer support—methods that traditional institutions often overlook. Watching young women rebuild their lives, create community, and choose trust over cynicism taught me that the deepest learning occurs not through information transfer but through relationships, not through curriculum but through courage.

Yet here's the problem: While AI can now process centuries of psychological research in seconds, it cannot sit with a recovering teenager and help her remember her own power. While quantum computers solve problems in minutes that would take us millennia, they cannot teach participants how to forgive. The most essential human learning—the kind that transforms lives and communities—still occurs the way it always has: through authentic connection, shared struggle, and the quiet courage of humans helping one another remember who they truly are.

Looking back at my traditional classroom days, I see the same barriers to authentic learning everywhere. I regularly visit schools where teenagers memorize facts about kings and queens and weather systems they'll forget within weeks—students preparing for tests that measure nothing meaningful about their ability to understand the world around them. The contrast with my nomadic experiences from over a decade outside the system was devastating.

One approach created lasting wisdom through authentic human experience: standing in front of nature, learning from survivors who had transformed trauma into strength, and discovering ancient truths through personal journeys. The other produced disposable knowledge that would die before graduation.

But here's what should concern you more than AI winning Nobel Prizes: brilliant people becoming irrelevant while still believing they're valuable. Research for this book fell at the exact period when artificial intelligence began to transform firms. Knowing what this book was about, friends and colleagues called me to share their experiences, some of them in tears. Entire departments dissolved overnight or existed in constant fear—not because of budget cuts, but because 26-year-olds with AI training were producing better strategic analysis and plans in two hours than teams with twenty years of experience could in two weeks. One asked me, "Did our expertise just become worthless?"

Another colleague, sadly released from a technology position, told me, "I kept thinking my experience would protect me. I was wrong."

A wave of corporate restructuring, driven by a strategic pivot towards artificial intelligence, accelerated through 2023 and has continued into 2024. In 2023 alone, the tech industry saw more than 260,000 jobs eliminated.[4] This trend was not simply about cost-cutting; it coincided with a massive reallocation of resources toward AI. For instance, in early 2023, Microsoft announced it would cut 10,000 jobs just as it deepened its multi-billion-dollar investment in OpenAI.[5] That same year, BuzzFeed shuttered its news division, with CEO Jonah Peretti announcing the company would "lean into AI and creators for content generation.[6]" By the end of 2024, despite heavy AI investment and launching an AI-driven social platform, the company's revenues continued to decline—a reminder that replacing human journalists with algorithms doesn't guarantee success.[7]

Then there's the suburban school district I visited that spent a huge percentage of its budget on developing a "revolutionary" new curriculum, minus any focus on teaching AI. By the time the AI tutor was launched at a rival school, they were sharing data that their tutors were teaching the same concepts better, faster, and more personalized to each student. The suburban curriculum committee still meets monthly. Nobody (yet) mentions that their work is already obsolete.

The cruelest part? These aren't lazy people or bad organizations. They are smart, dedicated professionals often trapped in systems built for a previous era, playing by rules that are quickly becoming obsolete.

The scale of the coming shift is immense. The World Economic Forum warned in 2020 that half of all employees would require significant reskilling by 2025.[8] The rise of generative AI has only accelerated this trend. A 2024 report from the McKinsey Global Institute now estimates that the technology could automate work activities that absorb 60% to 70% of employees' time today, urging companies to race to raise skills.[9] While legacy organizations operate on five-year cycles and multi-year training schedules, someone with a laptop and AI is solving problems they haven't even identified yet.

Every month you wait to adapt is six months behind in the new reality. Every year your organization delays transformation is a decade of catch-up time. The cost isn't just falling behind—it's becoming so irrelevant that catching up becomes impossible.

The urgent need for continuous learning is now undeniable. While a famous 2017 forecast once speculated that 85% of 2030's jobs had not yet been invented, a more concrete reality has emerged: The value of our existing skills is depreciating at an unprecedented rate.[10] Again, citing the World Economic Forum, they highlight the declining "half-life of skills," now estimating this to be less than five years for many professions and even shorter for specific technical competencies.[11] This means a skill learned today may be only half as valuable in five years. If this accelerated skill decay doesn't wake us up to the pace of change, nothing will. Yet, most of our educational and corporate training systems still operate on slow, linear cycles, as if we have decades to prepare for a future that is already here.

That contrast between wisdom and information, between living knowledge and dead facts, has shaped my understanding of what real education should be.

I see evidence of this disconnect everywhere. Take the conference I spoke at celebrating 'twenty-first-century educational innovation'—hundreds of teachers, thousands of dollars spent on technology, and presentations promising revolutionary approaches to learning.

As I listened to speaker after speaker, I noticed a deep fragmentation between the technology they promoted and the educational domains they claimed to serve. Peculiarly, despite all the talk of innovation, I realized we were still trapped in the same fundamental assumptions that created our broken system in the first place.

It occurred to me—with the force of a well-aimed brick—that we need to press the emergency button and start building practical solutions. However messy these solutions might feel at first, they are becoming essential. We need systems that support self-regulated learning by understanding how humans and artificial intelligence can truly coexist, frameworks that determine optimal levels of human-AI collaboration rather than replacement.

We need what I call "hybrid intelligence"—systematic approaches that determine whether human-machine collaboration actually serves the greater good. However, I'm growing concerned that we're just putting digital band-aids on Industrial Age wounds.

The most transformative learning I've witnessed has happened far from any conference room: watching students test their resilience on the six-day Inca Trail in Peru's Sacred Valley; seeing young people in tech-free Botswana discover new realities while wrestling with the complex relationship between humans and wildlife; observing Dubai's Rahhal program in the United Arab Emirates, an early attempt at proving the future of education, where students learn part-time across multiple schools, even hobbies can become legitimate qualifications, and "all learning that takes place both in and outside classrooms," and this is all officially recognized. Unique initiatives and experiences such as these propel teams toward building new systems, not patching old ones.

As I traveled through various countries, conducting learning expeditions, we sought authenticity. We found it most powerfully in Botswana's delta—bucket showers, tents, complete disconnection from devices, and family. There, young people discovered their resilience as they confronted harsh realities. The harsh realities of the delta's grueling heat, mosquitoes and their signature buzz—especially in the silence of a Botswana night, which can transform a peaceful evening into a state of low-level warfare—and the bone-deep exhaustion that strips away not just the ability to move but the memory of why movement was ever considered desirable, leaving one to regard the snail's pace as an almost offensive display of bravado.

In Botswana's wilderness, our team discovered more than just adventure. Each evening, local voices lifted in song welcomed us to dinner. Around crackling fires, rangers shared their raw, honest stories, often stuck in the thin khaki line between rhino and Kalashnikov—the daily battles against poaching, the economics of extinction, and the weight of protecting endangered wildlife—enriching us with their fears and triumphs.

These weren't just guides; they were guardians sharing hard-won wisdom. Their vulnerability and strength touched something deep in our learners, creating memories that outlasted any safari sighting.

Even in challenging terrain, we found ourselves anchored by human connection—experiences that transform long after the journey ends.

Away from the Kalahari's harsh beauty, the young people we partnered with across other continents faced different but equal realities—commercial and sexual exploitation, grinding poverty, and the relentless pressure of social media to define their worth. The educators and mentors I met in Kolkata, Cusco, and Panama City taught me more about resilience and creating alternatives within broken systems than any seminar or conference workshop ever could.

Real learning involves the allure of the unknown, complex, and confusing. I found myself alongside my learners, living a nomadic life where very little was guaranteed or predictable. I realized that deep learning happens in places that would never make it onto PowerPoint presentations or traditional curriculum timetables. So often, we defined this generation as digital natives, but what I saw was what Patrick Noack describes as "digital captives." [12]

What would set them free, I realized, wasn't more technology, better apps, or smarter algorithms. It was remembering how to learn like human beings again, with curiosity as their real compass, real problems as their curriculum, and authentic community as their classroom. That's when I knew I had to write this book. We need to be reminded that humans are already "natural-born cyborgs."

As cognitive scientist Andy Clark argues, what makes us uniquely human is our capacity to fully incorporate tools into our existence.[13] From writing on cave walls to Googling on smartphones, we think and feel through our technologies. The line between user and tool has always been thin; AI just makes this partnership more visible and more powerful.

We've always been hybrid thinking systems, fluidly incorporating non-biological resources from Stone Age tools to smartphones. So, learn, live, lead, and thrive alongside AI. We're not creating something entirely new, but we need to consciously design what we've always done intuitively.

The question that keeps me awake isn't how to improve education or our workplace, but how do we completely redesign learning for a world that's changing faster than our ability to adapt?

Here's what I've witnessed that most people never see. I've watched brilliant minds flourish in environments that would be considered failures by traditional standards. I've seen teenagers in remote communities solve complex problems while their peers in prestigious schools struggle with basic critical thinking. I've worked with corporations spending millions on training that changes very little, while other organizations transform entire cultures with simple shifts in how they approach learning, living, leading, thriving, and helping all these things grow.

We're standing at the threshold of a world where human creativity is our ultimate competitive advantage precisely because artificial intelligence has transformed, or will transform, every other domain. Imagine learning spaces that adapt to your unique cognitive patterns, where boundaries between teacher and student dissolve into collaborative discovery, intergenerational communities form around shared challenges, and wisdom flows in all directions.

My research and work across the globe have led me to ask whether a society could emerge in which giving 70% becomes the norm, where efficiency and focused excellence matter only when they truly count, and where the rest of life becomes experimental play, conscious exploration, and joyful discovery. However, this transformation won't happen automatically. It requires us to understand something profound about how learning works, something I discovered by studying one of nature's most remarkable phenomena: the firefly.

Many years ago, while facilitating a remote term during my nomadic existence in Costa Rica, I witnessed something that changed how I think about learning forever. Hundreds, if not thousands, of fireflies began to flash in the trees around our teacher dorm and classrooms, on a porch where, in the evenings, we would sit, have coffee, and watch the sunset. At first, the flashes seemed random, individual lights sparking sporadically in the darkness, but as I watched more carefully, because there was very little else to do, I noticed something extraordinary happening: night after night, the fireflies were synchronizing.

One would trigger another, then another, until an entire tree pulsed with coordinated light. No central command, no hierarchy, no external control, just authentic signals spreading through a living network. This was one of the moments when I realized how real learning could actually work: not through standardized inputs and measured outputs, but through authentic sparks that ignite other sparks; not through external motivation, but through self-generated light that synchronizes with others; not through isolated individual performance, but through collaborative illumination that transforms entire communities.

AI can now write legal briefs, diagnose diseases, and create marketing campaigns better than most professionals, but it can't be curious, can't build authentic relationships, and can't navigate uncertainty with wisdom. The question isn't whether AI will replace you; it's whether you develop the uniquely human capabilities to make yourself irreplaceable. The firefly, therefore, became my metaphor for everything that's possible when we stop trying to control learning and start creating conditions for it to flourish naturally.

So, who's this book for? It's for everyone who is tired of pretending that the broken systems are working. You might be a parent watching your child's natural curiosity getting crushed by standardization. You might be an educator who went into teaching to inspire minds, but find yourself managing compliance instead. You might be a corporate leader frustrated that expensive training programs change very little, or an entrepreneur trying to build learning organizations in a world of constant change. You might be someone who senses that everything you were taught about success, careers, and skill development is quickly becoming obsolete, but you're not sure what comes next.

What you're feeling right now—that mix of frustration, hope, and uncertainty—is exactly right. It means you're paying attention.

So, why listen to me?

I hope I've earned the right to help contribute to this conversation, not through credentials or titles, but through years of experimenting with what actually works on learning frontiers around the world. Through decisions rooted in risk and, I hope, a degree of bravery, my team and I have redesigned what's possible in education, guided by inquiry and curiosity.

I struggled under real pressure. My team and students depended on my leadership in designing learning experiences years ahead of traditional models—tackling AI integration in China, blockchain projects in Panama, and environmental challenges in Botswana and India. We always tried to occupy the frontier, the hinterlands where few have dared to tread. Our nomadic squad mastered the art of creating transformative learning environments. In these spaces, students naturally wove AI, blockchain, and other emerging tools into their thinking—not because a syllabus required it, but because the real-world challenges demanded it.

As mentioned earlier, we discovered what cognitive scientist Andy Clark calls our "natural-born cyborg" nature—that humans have always been hybrid thinking systems, fluidly incorporating external resources, from stone tools to smartphones. Our students weren't just using technology; they were thinking and problem-solving through it, their minds extending seamlessly into digital tools while remaining grounded in authentic human relationships and real-world challenges.

What I learned through all this was the extraordinary power of presenting a **compelling frame** to an audience, group of learners, or team of designers. For example, this book began with a simple content page—just bullet points of what I hoped for you as the reader, a skeletal structure that became something we hope will reshape how you think about learning forever. It was my first chess move.

It's not enough to simply gather information or follow other people's methods. Instead, it's about frame building—creating the right lens through which to see possibilities and then activating the tools that bring those possibilities to life. This book is built around three fundamental capabilities that you'll need to master:

Learn. You'll discover how to generate curiosity, adapt at breakneck speed, and turn every experience into fuel for growth, not just consuming information but creating wisdom through authentic exploration and real-world application.

Lead. You'll learn to take ownership without waiting for permission, build solutions that actually solve problems, and create conditions where others can discover their own light, leading in a way that sparks transformation, not compliance.

Thrive. You'll develop the systems to sustain wonder over the decades, build communities that amplify your impact, and navigate uncertainty with confidence, not just surviving change but dancing with it.

You'll learn how to live alongside technology and artificial intelligence, which could enter so many areas of our lives. I also hope you'll learn to appreciate ancient wisdom and apply it to modern tools as you learn, lead, and thrive.

Each capacity builds on the other. You can't lead authentically without learning continuously. You can't thrive long-term unless learning becomes as natural as breathing. In the age of AI, these aren't just professional skills; they're survival skills for anyone who wants to remain uniquely, powerfully human.

We're preparing for a world where human creativity is our ultimate frontier, where bio-integrated devices enhance learning in real time, where quantum environments create educational experiences that we can barely imagine today. The firefly mindset does not simply equate to a fancy add-on but is an essential part of surviving and thriving in the future. I've lived in communities where learning happens without schools. I've worked in organizations that innovate without formal research and development departments, and I've witnessed transformations that existing frameworks and theories can't explain.

Most importantly, after traveling the world and being nomadic for so long, I've learned to combine ancient wisdom about how humans actually grow and develop with cutting-edge insights into what's possible in our changing world. What does this actually look like? Well, indigenous cultures have long understood the concept of seasonal learning, which involves intensive periods followed by periods of integration and rest.

This is my firefly cycle, and it mirrors the ancient rhythm of hunt, rest, reflect: hunt that sustained human development for millennia, now adapted to the digital age. Firefly thinking is a form of biomimicry, where nature's most effective learning system is applied to human development.

Many of today's most innovative companies, from Interface to Patagonia, have built their success on ancient ecological principles, proving that the oldest wisdom often yields the most effective solutions. This taps into a fundamental human truth: For two hundred thousand years, we have transferred complex knowledge through narrative, not data dumps. The most effective leaders instinctively understand this. They don't teach with presentations that fade; they lead with stories that stick.

Every framework in this book follows the same principle, wrapping complex ideas in what I hope are memorable stories. The Southern African concept of Ubuntu, "I am because we are," perfectly describes how modern learning networks function. Individual firefly sparks become powerful when synchronized with others, just as ancient communities shared knowledge for collective survival.

This book isn't about choosing between old and new; it's about weaving them together skillfully so that timeless principles amplify cutting-edge possibilities and modern tools honor ancient truths about how humans actually learn and grow. When you finish this book, I hope you'll carry a different understanding of what learning, leading, and living can be.

You'll have concrete tools for swift development, authentic community building, and sustainable growth that adapts to whatever changes come next. More than that, I hope you'll be able to become a spark yourself, someone who ignites curiosity in others.

Here's precisely what you'll be able to do after reading this book:

Within 24 hours, you'll be able to identify your first firefly experiment: a specific area where you'll stop waiting for permission and start building capability at unprecedented speed.

Within thirty days, you'll have dismantled at least one piece of performance theater in your life and replaced it with authentic learning that creates real value. You'll know how to spot fake innovation and invest your energy only in what generates genuine light.

Within ninety days, you'll be operating on firefly time, learning in six-month cycles what used to take five years, building solutions while others are still planning, and sparking transformation in your sphere of influence.

Most importantly, you'll stop being afraid of obsolescence. You'll have a repeatable system for staying ahead of change, turning uncertainty into opportunity, and helping others do the same. Whether AI transforms your industry tomorrow or in ten years, you'll be ready, not because you can predict the future but because you've mastered the art of adaptation.

This isn't self-help. This isn't motivation. This is a practical blueprint for thriving in a world where the only constant is acceleration.

I imagine that if just 1% of the people who read this book begin implementing firefly thinking in their own spheres of influence—for example, teachers creating classrooms where wonder matters more than test scores, parents fostering curiosities instead of compliance, and leaders building organizations where learning is continuous and joyful—it could lead to significant transformation.

That's not just individual transformation; it's the beginning of a movement, a shift from systems that dim human potential to communities that help every person discover and develop their unique light.

However, before we can create that future, we need to understand exactly how we got trapped in a system that works against our natural learning instincts. We need to examine why the old glow is flickering out and what's killing the curiosity and creativity we desperately need.

That's where our journey begins.

The Firefly Effect *is the phenomenon where individual acts of authentic, self-generated brilliance create cascading illumination across communities, transforming darkness into opportunity through synchronized yet autonomous action. It's the antidote to AI-era overwhelm; instead of competing with machines' computational power, humans become living beacons of creativity, wisdom, and connection.*

ARC ONE
THE BROKEN GLOW: WHY THE OLD SYSTEM FAILS

"If you always do what you've always done,
you'll always get what you've always got."
— Henry Ford

Before we can light new fires, we must understand the issues and some of the problems that have emerged. Why have old and outdated flames remained flickering, with new lights unable to glow? I want to say here that for decades, we've built learning, leadership, and systems that allow us to thrive on assumptions that make sense in a much slower world of limited technology and certainly without the tsunami of artificial intelligence.

For centuries, we assumed that knowledge was scarce and sacred, and many specific gatekeepers protected it, deciding whom to share it with and how. These gatekeepers included librarians, academic professors, guilds, and licensing bodies, which controlled qualifying exams and maintained exclusive access to technical information and best practices in their fields.

We also assumed that the future was largely predictable. This is why we are often obsessed with five- and ten-year plans. Our fixation on long-term planning reveals a deep human need for control and certainty, and we mistakenly believe that we can tame uncertainty through careful documentation and projection. The reality, however, is that this mode of thinking often makes organizations less adaptive, slower, and more ponderous when real change is needed. We assume that compliance and order are of the ultimate value, and we often look down on the contrarian.

It is not my intention to catastrophize the collapse of the old. Indeed, this is somewhat of an inevitable process, and has led us to an interesting paradox: The act of long-term planning could now realistically make organizations less prepared for the future. Energy wasted on elaborate predictions could have been spent on greater adaptive capacity. How many transformative moments were prevented because they did not fit into someone's five-year plan? There is a hidden cost: the silence of the contrarian, those who look where others are afraid to wander.

We are left to ponder:

- What if we measured organizational health not by adherence to plans but by speed of adaptation when plans prove to be wrong?
- How might our institutions have evolved differently if we had celebrated "productive contrarians," those who question not to destroy but to strengthen?
- Could AI help us distinguish between contrarianism that adds value rather than mere opposition?
- What would planning look like if we assumed unpredictability as the default rather than stability?
- How do we preserve the benefits of expertise and standards while avoiding the rigidity that made traditional gatekeepers vulnerable to disruption?

We've fallen into a trap of rewarding conformity over curiosity, and this has crept into many of the domains we occupy and value, including schools and universities, our professional careers, and even our relationships. However, the world has changed at an incredible speed. Our systems haven't kept up, and we need a new path forward—one that is positive, inspiring, and doesn't cast shadows.

The next three chapters set the stage for what has gone before so that we can understand where we are heading. We're going to examine the three pillars propping up the old system and why each one is crumbling.

Chapter 1: The Collapse of Time will examine the collapse of time, exploring how AI and exponential change have rendered long-term thinking largely obsolete and why agility is emerging as a key concept. While buzzwords such as "agility," "adaptiveness," and "flexibility" were often largely mocked as nonsense jargon used on resumes without any serious application, they are now essential parts of any strategy and skills that will always be in demand.

Chapter 2: The Great Pretend. What happens when twenty years of experience becomes a liability? The second chapter will focus on "The Great Pretend," the performance of theater that we see in almost all facets of life, where everyone knows the system is broken, but they keep applauding anyway. We will also examine how billions of dollars are wasted on learning and experiences that never actually occur. Is this a survival mechanism? Do we keep applauding ourselves in a cycle of professional training because stopping would force us to confront a very uncomfortable reality?

We've become attached to "competent incompetence," and we've become extremely good at optimizing broken systems. This explains why intelligent people often perpetuate dysfunction and embark on side quests. Just as biological monocultures are vulnerable to disease, intellectual monocultures are vulnerable to disruption. Diversity isn't just fair—it's adaptive.

Chapter 3: The Testing Syndrome & the Death of Wonder we will explore what we call the "testing syndrome": how our obsession with measurement has killed wonder. Standardization and the need to fit a mold have stifled and diminished creativity, which we desperately need to solve some of humanity's most challenging problems. Optimizing compliance and accumulating rules and systems have largely repelled, not rewarded, innovation.

This isn't about tearing everything down. We can certainly honor ancient wisdom, indigenous knowledge, and the wonderful things that have emerged from the Industrial Revolution and subsequent periods. However, I think we need to shine a much deeper light on what we've actually built, perhaps with a more critical lens, because the need for agility is crucial. We can't fix what we won't face, and we can't build something new on the foundations that pre-exist.

The broken glow isn't your fault. It isn't anyone's fault, but fixing it is our responsibility. So we need to start with the hardest truth of all: It's time things changed, as time itself has changed, and most of us are still living in the past.

CHAPTER 1

THE COLLAPSE OF TIME: WHEN SPEED BEATS EXPERIENCE

"Roads? Where we're going, we don't need roads."

— Doc Brown, *Back to the Future* (1985)

Signal from the Future*: A mother watches her 8-year-old complete her entire third-grade curriculum in six weeks through AI-guided learning. The school board meets for the fifth time this year to debate whether to keep the traditional September-to-June calendar. The mother has already enrolled her daughter in a technology-free marine biology apprenticeship at the local beach that starts next month.*

Picture yourself in the heart of ancient Athens, when it was the beating center of civilization. The Agora pulses with life—merchants hawking their wares, philosophers debating in the shade, citizens conducting the business of democracy. The sun tracks across the sky, casting shifting shadows that serve as the only timepiece most Athenians need. No one checks their wrist. No one rushes to make the 2:30 p.m. meeting. Time flows, measured in broad strokes by sundials and water clocks, but never sliced into the anxious minutes that rule our modern existence.

This image captivated me during my years traversing the globe as an educator and then leader of the world's first traveling school. In Athens, I stood with my students among the ruins where Socrates once questioned everything, and we reflected on something profound: the people who laid the foundations of Western thought had no concept of exact time. They navigated their days by shadows and seasons, yet somehow managed to tackle philosophy's deepest questions, build architectural marvels, and create art that still moves us millennia later.

THE PRISON OF PRECISION

Fast forward to today, where time has become our master rather than our tool. We've built entire civilizations around the clock—nine-to-five workdays, four-year degrees, five-year strategic plans. Time has become our credential. "I've been teaching for thirty years," we say, as if duration alone confers wisdom. "Twenty years of experience in the field," reads the LinkedIn profile, demanding deference.

We've mistaken rigidity for stability, not realizing that time-based hierarchies only work when knowledge moves slowly. But systems are fragile and can quickly become obsolete.

What happens when time itself begins to collapse?

I watched as artificial intelligence entered every domain of our world. Was it an intruder or a welcome guest? The schools I was guiding differed in opinion. Many saw it as dangerous, but there was a sense of its inevitability. Schools were seeing their seventeen- and eighteen-year-olds coding applications that would have taken teams of engineers months to build just a decade ago. Some were even designing platforms, medical applications, and financial and blockchain interfaces. They would become company founders in their early 20s, achieving in two years what previous generations needed decades to accomplish. Their success wasn't measured in time served but in problems solved, value created, and impact delivered.

What would the reaction be when teachers realized that decades of expertise and experience were suddenly equaled by an AI agent with infinite patience and no concern for religion, gender, class, or ethnicity? I pondered how we would tell this story. Sure, some would race ahead, but many would also be left behind.

The old equation—time invested equals expertise gained—was crumbling before my eyes.

The Collapse of Time
From Industrial Age Rhythms to Firefly Speed
TRADITIONAL TIME
Linear • Predictable • Hierarchical
30-Year Careers
One company, one path, gold watch retirement
4-Year Degrees
Fixed curriculum, rigid prerequisites
5-Year Strategic Plans
Long-term predictions, detailed roadmaps
Annual Performance Reviews
Yearly cycles, slow feedback loops
Skills Last Decades
Learn once, apply for entire career
Continuous steady burn
FIREFLY TIME
Cyclical • Adaptive • Networked
18-Month Skill Expiration
Constant reinvention, perpetual learning
6-Month Learning Cycles
Spark → Flash → Converge → Glow → Rest
72-Hour Prototypes
Build fast, fail fast, learn faster
Continuous Iteration
Real-time adaptation, instant feedback
Flash-and-Rest Patterns
Intense bursts, regenerative pauses
Intermittent synchronized flashes
"Time served is no longer the credential. What matters now is what you can do with knowledge."

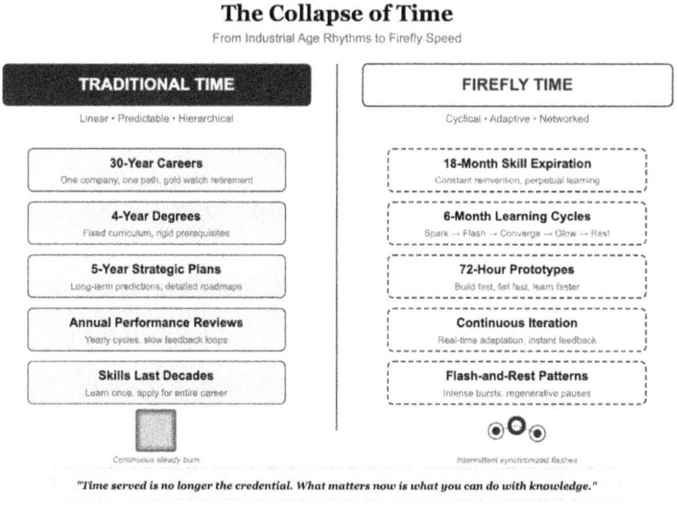

Figure 1: The Time Collapse Comparison - From Industrial Age Rhythms to Firefly Speed. This side-by-side comparison reveals the fundamental shift in how time operates in the age of AI. Traditional Time (left) shows the linear, predictable structures that organized human life for generations: 30-year careers, 4-year degrees, 5-year plans. Firefly Time (right) shows our new reality: 18-month skill expiration, six-month learning cycles, 72-hour prototypes. The visual metaphor captures the essence—where traditional time burns steadily like a candle, firefly time flashes in brilliant, intermittent bursts. This isn't just acceleration; it's a different relationship with time itself.

THE SHOCK FACTOR

It was March 2020, Panama City. Casco Viejo, the Old Town, was buzzing with life: people gathered in the central square, the rooftops were alive, and locals and internationals mixed as the shops closed and the bars and restaurants came to life.

After the nomadic school term had ended, I had decided to stay a couple of extra nights. I was eager to help a local school adopt a more student-centered approach to learning, and on a personal level, I had enjoyed my experience so far; I had a fairly fancy Airbnb and was keen to stay on for a while. Rumors of the virus had been reported on the BBC, CNN, and other networks. *A virus in China reaching Panama? Not a chance,* I remember thinking.

How wrong I was.

We all have our personal stories about this period.

For me, time seemed to blur around this stage of my life. The shops and restaurants fell silent; words like "curfew," "social distancing," and "lockdown" entered our lexicon in the most intrusive way possible.

Our curfew was 5:00 p.m. One hour a day, three times a week, we were allowed outside for essentials.

Little did I know that three months later, while I was on an evacuation flight to Frankfurt, the world would be forever changed. My personal ordeal of house confinement was over, but our whole business model as a traveling school had come to a halt. Learning moved online, guest speakers became talking heads on Zoom calls, and we all had to get creative. Online quizzes gained popularity, we changed our virtual backgrounds to keep things fresh, binge-watched seasons of shows on Netflix, collectively experienced the Chicago Bulls through *The Last Dance* documentary, and cobbled together home gyms from whatever we could find. There was no end in sight.

In my professional world, time had collapsed, as had our strategy. I was watching the world reshape itself through my laptop screen, knowing as a leader that I needed to reinvent our whole model and approach to learning. In just a few weeks, the next term, now online, would begin.

Eventually, the pandemic came to an end, and the world began to recover. However, our five-year plan, which we had so proudly submitted to our school accreditation body the year before, was not only obsolete but almost entirely and embarrassingly redundant.

The pandemic had rendered almost every projection obsolete. Companies and schools closed overnight or moved online, and we distinguished between essential and non-essential services. We were confined to our homes, and relationships and coexistence entered a new reality. All the carefully built timelines, strategic roadmaps, and phased implementations were now worthless in a new world that had undergone a fundamental shift.

Just as organizations were catching their breaths, another shockwave hit: ChatGPT burst onto the scene, democratizing access to condensed human knowledge. Suddenly, anyone with an internet connection could access centuries of learning in milliseconds. As a history teacher by trade, I watched in awe as AI could not only summarize World War I in seconds but also create diary entries from the perspectives of Churchill, Mussolini, and Stalin; explain trench warfare through a soldier's eyes; and synthesize complex historical patterns that would take human researchers months to uncover.

These weren't isolated disruptions. They were instabilities that signaled a new reality where long-term planning had become an antique. Our once treasured planning documents and strategies were sundials in a digital age.

THE FIREFLY PRINCIPLE

This brings us to the firefly—nature's master of short, impactful bursts.

Fireflies don't glow constantly; they flash brilliantly for mere seconds, communicating everything necessary in those brief moments of illumination. They embody what our institutions must become: organisms built for cycles of brilliance rather than the slow burn of accumulated time.

Look at the evidence already emerging, the landscape in which firefly thinking becomes an essential tool of existence, not a nice-to-have:

TikTok has built a $16 billion empire in five years, while traditional media companies have taken decades to reach similar valuations.

Midjourney evolved from version one to version six in two years, outpacing entire industries that measure progress in decades.

OpenAI compressed centuries of language evolution into models that iterate on cycles measured in months, not years.

The pattern is unmistakable: The new giants operate on firefly time—short, intense bursts of innovation that create more value than decades of steady progress.

FIREFLY FLASHPOINT

If skills do start to expire every 18 months,
why should we continue to fund four-year degrees?

THE SIX-MONTH SPRINT

But here's where it gets interesting: even these established design companies are discovering that their most transformative moments come in firefly flashes. LEGO's breakthrough IDEAS platform, McKinsey's five-day concept sprints, IDEO's rapid prototyping—innovations are emerging not from the ten-year plans but from the intense bursts of creativity those plans enable.

This isn't just about technology companies. During the pandemic, vaccine development—traditionally a five-year process—was compressed to six to eight months. When human urgency demanded it, when survival was at stake, we discovered that our careful timelines were more about comfort than necessity.

Here's what should concern you: A 2023 study found that GPT-4 now outperforms humans on standardized tests of creative potential, scoring in the top 1% for originality.[14] We spent decades training children to think like machines, just as machines learned to out-create us.

The irony would be funny if it weren't so devastating.

The question emerges: Are six-month cycles more human? Are they more aligned with nature's rhythms of seasons and growth? The firefly doesn't require strategic planning sessions or five-year roadmaps. It simply flashes when the moment is right, trusting its inner chemistry to create connection.

DISMANTLING HIERARCHIES

This collapse of time as currency threatens every hierarchy we've built. The senior professor with three decades of experience suddenly finds herself on equal footing with the graduate student who can prompt AI to synthesize those same decades of knowledge in minutes. The executive who climbed the corporate ladder for twenty years watches as entrepreneurs in their twenties build and sell companies before he's finished his five-year strategic plan.

"You've only been here six months—what could you possibly know?" becomes a question as odd as asking for the exact time in ancient Athens. In an AI-augmented world, the novice with the right questions might contribute more than the veteran with outdated answers.

This isn't to say that experience has no value. Wisdom, judgment, and pattern recognition—these remain crucial. But they're no longer monopolies held by those who've simply existed in a role the longest. Time served is no longer the primary credential. What matters now is what you can do with knowledge, not how long you've been accumulating it.

I find myself reconsidering every mentoring relationship I've had. Do they invert completely? Do they become bidirectional exchanges? Or are we witnessing the birth of something entirely new—a form of mutual learning we don't yet have words for?

EDUCATION'S EXTINCTION EVENT

Perhaps nowhere is this temporal collapse more disruptive than in the education sector. Why does a bachelor's degree require four years? Why do we still march students through twelve grades when AI can personalize learning at the speed of thought?

One example of this is Alpha School, which offers a glimpse of the future: two hours of AI-assisted core learning, with the rest of the day spent on real-world projects. Many will ask, "Is two hours enough for core learning?" Alpha School says yes—as founder McKenzie Price commented on a recent Fox7 report: "Under 2-Hour Learning, our results are incredible. Our students are in the top 2% in the country in how they're learning."[15]

Homeschooling has become the fastest-growing form of education in the United States. An analysis of U.S. Census Bureau data by The Washington Post revealed that the number of homeschooled children surged by more than 50% between 2019 and the 2022-2023 school year, representing a fundamental shift in the American educational landscape.[16]

The three-year degree, the semester system, the gap year—all are relics of an era when knowledge moved at the speed of printing presses, not fiber-optic cables.

Unless we're testing something other than knowledge acquisition—patience, perhaps, or conformity to temporal structures—the traditional timelines of education make no sense in an era of instant access to humanity's accumulated wisdom. We are witnessing a collapse of traditional timelines and structures.

FIREFLY FLASHPOINT

Here's an uncomfortable truth: Many "innovations" are just faster paths to the same dead end. The real challenge isn't catching up to the latest trend; it's jumping tracks entirely to a new way of thinking.

THE VUCA REALITY

Futurists speak of our VUCA world—Volatile, Uncertain, Complex, and Ambiguous. In such an environment, being chained to time-based structures isn't just inefficient; it's dangerous.

While VUCA has its critics, some argue it's become outdated in our AI and post-pandemic era, preferring newer frameworks like BANI (Brittle, Anxious, Nonlinear, Incomprehensible)—it remains the most widely recognized way to describe our current reality. What matters isn't the acronym we choose, but acknowledging that our world resists the tidy categories and timelines we try to impose on it.

Perhaps Heraclitus said it best 2,500 years ago: "Nothing is permanent except change." The ancient philosopher would have instantly recognized our VUCA world, not as something new, but as the fundamental nature of existence we've been trying to deny with our five-year plans and tenure tracks.

Therefore, our aim should be to ensure that what rises in its place is something more dynamic, responsive, and alive.

Although there seems to be something deeply psychological about our attachment to time-based structures, they often give us an illusion of progress even when we're standing still. However, this shift from time as a compass to time as a prison terrifies us. We've built so much on time-based foundations:

- Retirement after forty years
- Tenure after seven
- Promotions based on time in grade
- Degrees that take prescribed years to complete

To abandon time as our primary organizing principle is to dismantle a century of institutional architecture. However, questions remain. Despite their flaws, do time-based systems provide some degree of democratic opportunity, allowing everyone to move at firefly speed, or will this favor certain personalities and circumstances? Some might claim that living in a perpetual, volatile, uncertain, complex, and ambiguous world without its time-based anchoring sounds exhausting. If so, what would sabbaticals look like in a firefly world?

Also, is this about losing our structures, or is it about losing a shared mythology of progress—the forty-year career, the gold watch, the tenure celebration? These stories are meaningful, and maybe we are not ready to let them go.

It's little wonder we resist, even as the evidence mounts that our temporal structures are crumbling.

RACING TOWARD THE DIVIDE

We're approaching an inevitable split. Some institutions, like Duolingo, have declared themselves "AI-first" companies, embracing the collapse of traditional timelines. They'll operate on firefly time: iterate fast, fail rapidly, and succeed even more quickly. Others will dig in, banning AI, checking every assignment for plagiarism, and insisting on near-total commitment to their four-year programs and five-year plans.

I graduated from university in 2000, yet if I walk into almost any lecture hall internationally, I will see rows of students, 50-minute blocks, and professors teaching a set curriculum. Now, how might an AI-first institution look? Students collaborating with AI tutors, completing coursework in weeks, not semesters, and tackling real projects the moment they grasp the big concepts. If done right, the contrast becomes existential.

Pragmatists will argue they're taking a balanced approach, but often, this is just a cover for resistance. In the real world, we're already seeing AI-enhanced incubators emerge in schools—test beds and gentle starts to what the future may hold, a place in the curriculum where some risk feels palatable to parents and observers. No plan is without casualties.

At what point does the risk invert? When does not doing AI become a greater risk than abandoning what we've called "core skills"? Perhaps that tipping point has already passed, and we're just too attached to our temporal structures to see it.

The question isn't whether they're right or wrong to resist. The question is whether their resistance comes from strategic wisdom—preserving something precious about human-paced learning—or from simply burying their heads in the sand. Parents, students, and employees will soon vote with their feet, choosing institutions that match the tempo of our accelerating world.

Perhaps the great irony here is that both sides of this divide are trying to preserve something essential about human potential. One believes that potential is best realized through careful cultivation over time. The other believes it's best unleashed through rapid iteration and AI augmentation. The tragedy isn't that they disagree—it's that they may both be right, and we're forcing ourselves to choose.

OPPORTUNITY HIDDEN IN COLLAPSE

Let's not view this only as destruction or an impossible choice. The collapse of time offers profound opportunities:

- **De-extinction scientists** operating on agile prototyping cycles are bringing back species we thought lost forever—dire wolves currently, and potentially Tasmanian tigers and woolly mammoths. Teams such as those at Colossal Bioscience now work in months, not decades.

- **Environmental solutions** that might have taken generations to develop now emerge in shortened cycles, as AI helps us model complex systems and test interventions at unprecedented speed.
- **Medical breakthroughs** accelerate as researchers compress decades of trial and error into months of AI-assisted discovery. AlphaFold, a groundbreaking AI system developed by DeepMind, which is Google's AI subsidiary, cracked a fifty-year protein folding puzzle in just two years, potentially revolutionizing drug discovery overnight. To add to the list, in 2021, DeepMind released predictions for two hundred million proteins, nearly every protein known to science.

When we're freed from the tyranny of time-based hierarchies, we can finally ask the right questions: What can you do? What problems can you solve? What value can you create?

Not: How long have you been here?

LIVING AT LIGHT SPEED

Ask yourself, what do you believe about time now that you didn't believe ten years ago? If your answer is nothing, you might already be falling behind.

Why?

This new world demands new skills.

Adaptability, once dismissed as mere resume jargon, has become essential for survival. The ability to learn, unlearn, and relearn at firefly speed separates those who thrive from those who merely endure. Twenty years of experience might actually become a liability if those years trained you in patterns that no longer apply.

History is littered with cautionary tales. Kodak commanded 90% of the film market and 85% of the camera market, and it even invented the digital camera in 1975. However, its culture of risk aversion and reluctance to change made adaptation impossible. Middle managers, rigid bureaucratic systems, and decades of film expertise became anchors dragging them down. By 2012, Kodak filed for bankruptcy—their century of experience worthless in the digital age.[17]

Today's tech layoffs echo this pattern. Engineers with decades at Microsoft or Amazon send out a thousand applications without success, while those fluent in AI tools leap ahead. When your patterns no longer align with reality, experience transforms from an asset to an anchor.

However, speed without wisdom is merely frenzy. As we race toward this temporally collapsed future, we need mechanisms to pause, reflect, and ensure that we're running toward something, not just away from the past.

What strategies can help us slow down in a world moving at light speed?

Perhaps the answer lies in those ancient Athenians, who had all the time in the world because they weren't counting it. They focused on depth over duration, wisdom over credentials, and genuine inquiry over prescribed timelines. In our rush to compress time, we might rediscover what they knew: The most profound insights emerge not from racing against the clock but from occasionally forgetting it exists.

The broken glow of our temporal structures offers a choice. We can frantically try to repair the old timelines, insisting that four-year degrees and five-year plans still make sense—the roads we've always traveled. Or we can embrace the firefly's wisdom: shine brilliantly in the moment, adapt to conditions as they are, create value in intensive bursts rather than extensive duration. Roads? Where we're going, we don't need roads.

Time, which was once our organizing principle, has become our prison. The question isn't whether we'll escape—the walls are already crumbling. The question is what we'll build in the light of our new freedom.

REGENERATIVE MOMENT

Before you turn to the next chapter, put this book down. Set a timer for 60 seconds—yes, we're using time to escape time. Close your eyes. Take three deep breaths, each one slower than the last.

Ask yourself: *What would I create if I had only six months?* Not six years, not a lifetime—six months. What problem would I solve? What impact would I make? What would I build if I embraced the firefly's wisdom of brilliant, brief illumination?

When the timer rings, notice how different a minute feels when you're not racing through it. That's the paradox we must master: moving at light speed while carrying stillness within.

The future belongs to those who can dance between velocity and reflection, who can compress decades into moments while expanding moments into lifetimes. The fireflies are showing us the way.

Time's up. Time to begin.

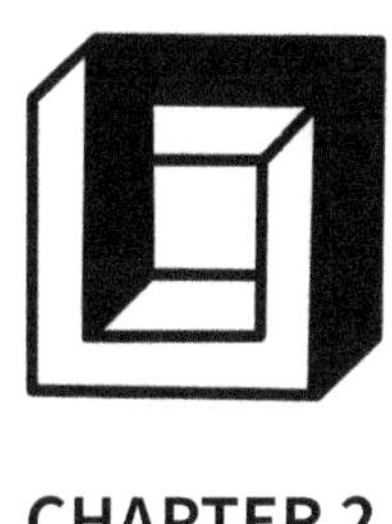

CHAPTER 2

THE GREAT PRETEND: PERFORMANCE OVER PROGRESS

"We pretend to work, and they pretend to pay us."
— Soviet-era saying

Signal from the Future: *At the office, holographic executives deliver passionate speeches about "authentic human connection" to empty conference rooms while every actual employee works from home. The AI-generated avatars don't notice they're performing for security cameras and cleaning robots.*

THE UNDERGROUND TRUTH

In Rome's underground ruins, I discovered something that would change my perspective on the distinction between performance and reality.

Picture this: 1480, Rome's Oppian Hill. As diggers search for the Baths of Titus, suddenly, the earth swallows one of them. Crashing through dirt, through time, he lands hard in ancient rubble. But when he lifts his torch and looks up, there it is: a ceiling dripping with frescoes, sumptuous and untouched, as if the artist had just stepped away. He'd fallen into Nero's lost palace.

Descending into the Domus Aurea felt like discovering a vast network of rooms hidden beneath Rome's everyday bustle, accessible only to those who knew where to look. Our small group, feeling like archaeologists and explorers, walked the same halls as Emperor Nero.

"Imagine thinking you're exploring a cave," our guide said, pointing to a centuries-old breach in the ceiling, "only to realize you're standing in the hallways of power that once ruled the known world. Michelangelo himself came down through a hole right about here."

The irony wasn't lost on me. Nero had built this pleasure palace after the great fire of 64 AD. Sprawling across acres that had belonged to thousands of displaced citizens, its construction was an example of the ultimate performance of leadership, though some might argue it exemplified the failure to actually lead. Virtual reality headsets might soon let tourists see reconstructions of the original grandeur, much like they do for the ancient Pyramids—the revolving dining rooms, walls that sprayed perfume. But as we stood in the actual space, breathing the air that Michelangelo had once breathed, touching walls that Renaissance hands had discovered, the experience carried a weight no reconstruction could match.

The Romans called it *"damnatio memoriae,"* attempting to erase Nero and his excesses from history after his death. But here's what struck me as we stood in those once-buried halls: Every generation builds its own palaces of pretense. The surfaces might dazzle, but sometimes, the foundations rot.

WELCOME TO KAYFABE

There's a term in professional wrestling that I need you to understand: "kayfabe." It's the elaborate storytelling where reality and fiction blur together, where everyone knows it's staged but plays along anyway.

The genius of kayfabe lies in its proximity to truth, mixing real athletic skill and genuine injuries with scripted outcomes. This makes us believe we're witnessing something authentic even when we all know it's a show.

Sound familiar? Welcome to modern institutional life.

Remember watching wrestling as a child? That ongoing debate—is it real or fake? Like discovering the truth about Santa Claus, there's a moment when you realize it's staged, then another moment when you understand that everyone knows it's staged, yet we all continue the performance. No one breaks character. That's the brilliance and the tragedy.

Kayfabe isn't confined to the wrestling ring. It's everywhere. Many questions have emerged since: Why do we want to be fooled? Why do we play along? And why does such a performance create such an emotional reaction? Some love the performance, knowing it's fake but relishing the disappointment, the cynicism, and then the enjoyment.

Here's the truly disturbing part: Once you see kayfabe everywhere, you can't unsee it. Every corporate all-hands, every graduation ceremony, every performance review—they all start to look like wrestling matches, complete with predetermined outcomes and rehearsed drama.

THE EDUCATIONAL CHARADE

Walk into almost any school today and witness the performance. Students sit in rows—a formation invented for factories, not minds. Bells ring to signal transitions like we're still punching time clocks. Teachers, many of whom are brilliant and dedicated, are forced to "teach to the test" while knowing that these standardized measurements capture little of real intelligence or creativity.

I've spent years working with schools, training teachers, and designing curricula. The disconnect between what we say we want and what we actually do would be comedic if it weren't so tragic. Ask any parent what they want their child to get from school. My experience with parents aligns with that of the education reformer Alfie Kohn. When he asks in his talks what parents want from education, the answers are always "I want them to be happy," "I want them to enjoy learning," and "I want them to make meaningful connections."

Never once have I heard, "I want them to score perfectly on standardized tests."

Yet the entire system optimizes for test scores. We know it's a joke. The teachers know. The students know. The parents know. But we all play along.

On one school visit, a teacher told me about her school's VR rollout several years before—the supposed revolution in learning. "I thought it would change everything," she said with a sigh, sounding fairly beaten up, even demoralized. "But the kids were just bored. They go home to play games that are a thousand times more sophisticated. We're always drowning in the next big update that promises transformation but delivers more worksheets or something they can access outside these four walls."

Remembering the noise around virtual reality was a powerful reflective moment for me. During my career in education, I often found myself asking, "Will VR trigger a revolution? Will it trigger what AI has basically done?" The answer, ultimately, has been no. The Apple Vision Pro never caught fire; the price point and accessibility were beyond many, and education or corporate training didn't have an appetite for it.

During the same visit, the self-proclaimed innovator running the evening professional development session—wearing an oversized blazer and employing rehearsed TED talk gestures—kept talking about "embracing disruption" while delivering the most traditional, top-down training imaginable. The irony was lost on him, but not on the exhausted teachers who'd seen this performance before.

The fascination for me as an observer was that the innovator probably believed he was an innovator and that he was disruptive. Unlike wrestlers, who know they are part of an act, many in the corporate world have convinced themselves that their act is real. There is almost a deeper tragedy in this.

I asked myself, *How insidious is this act?* The commercialization of change, selling "disruption" while reinforcing the very systems that need disrupting—it's kayfabe layered in kayfabe, performing the performance of innovation.

THE CORPORATE THEATER

The numbers are staggering: U.S. companies spent $101.8 billion on training in 2023,[18] yet only 27% of learning and development professionals even measure whether behaviors change after training.[19] Harvard Business School researchers call it "The Great Training Robbery" estimating that organizations waste $200 billion globally on training that doesn't stick.[20] When studies do track application, they find that while 62% of employees apply training immediately, this drops to just 34% after one year.[21] That's roughly $67 billion in vanishing value—pure performance theater.

If education perfected kayfabe, corporate culture made it an art form. Think of *The Office*—both Ricky Gervais's UK original and Steve Carell's USA version. The show's genius was recognizing that everyone knows the boss is incompetent, the metrics are meaningless, and the mission statements are empty. Yet we all respond to the hierarchy, attend pointless meetings, and nod through the professional development sessions. The show's creators set it in a paper company—a perfect metaphor for industries producing nothing while maintaining elaborate performances of productivity.

The Factory, by Hiroko Oyamada, is a particularly haunting example of this mindset.[22] In it, workers show up daily to a massive industrial complex, follow elaborate protocols, and maintain strict hierarchies, but here's the thing—no one really knows what they're producing. One character spends his days proofreading documents that may never be read. Another runs bizarre "training programs" for skills no one needs. A third catalogs moss growing on the factory grounds, treating it like vital work.

Everyone senses the absurdity. The workers exchange knowing glances, sharing an unspoken understanding that their labor produces nothing of value, yet they keep coming, keep performing their meaningless tasks with dedication that would be admirable if it weren't so tragic. The paychecks clear. The hierarchy provides structure. The performance continues.

Oyamada wrote this as satire, but as you'll see if you walk through any large corporation today, is it really fiction? How many employees can clearly connect their daily tasks to actual value creation? How many meetings exist solely to justify other meetings? How many reports get filed and forgotten?

The factory in Oyamada's book isn't just a building—it's a state of mind. It's every institution where the appearance of productivity matters more than productivity itself, where the performance of work has replaced work, where everyone knows but no one speaks.

In the United States version of *The Office,* the character Dwight Schrute III, played by the actor Rainn Wilson, lives so deeply in the kayfabe that he believes promotions come from perfect performance of the charade. The more enthusiastically you pretend, the more you'll be rewarded—except the rewards are just more elaborate roles and tasks in the same meaningless play.

THE INNOVATION ILLUSION

With every failed revolution comes greater demoralization. I've watched educators spend months "gamifying" their lessons and "reimagining" their curricula—those horrible buzzwords that mean little and change even less. Students glaze over because they've experienced real engagement—Call of Duty, Fortnite, TikTok. The gap between what happens on the technological frontier inside the institutional walls and outside them has never been wider.

A father once told me about confronting his son's principal. He'd enrolled his son expecting hands-on learning and real-world immersion—what the marketing materials had promised. What did he get? Worksheets. Traditional schedules. The same factory model wrapped in digital rhetoric.

"They promised me the future," he told me, his voice tinged with anger, "but my boy's just bored and doing worksheets, same as before."

Apparently, the principal had deflected him with buzzwords: "digital fluency," "twenty-first-century skills," "personalized learning pathways"—empty phrases signaling much but delivering nothing. The father had pulled his son out of the school the week before our meeting, joining the homeschooling exodus. "I'm sick of the jargon," he said. "At least at home, we're honest about what we're doing."

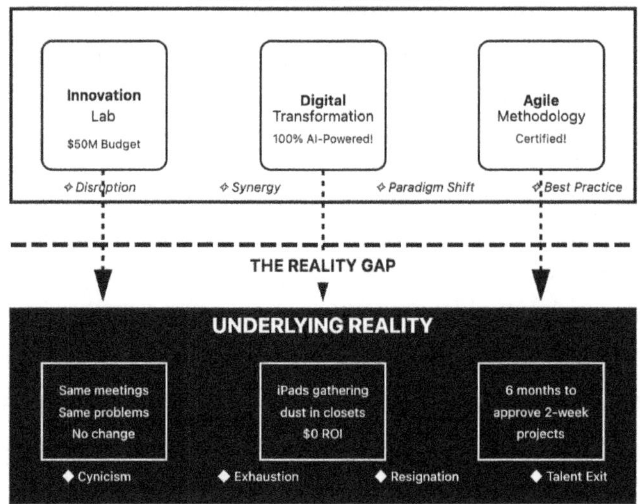

Figure 2: The Great Pretend - When Performance Replaces Progress - This diagram exposes the gap between innovation theater and organizational reality. The top level shows the bright, expensive performance—Innovation Labs, Digital Transformations, and Agile Methodologies with their impressive budgets and certifications. The dashed arrows reveal how each initiative maps to the dark reality below: unused tools, unchanged processes, and approval bottlenecks. The stark visual contrast between white performance and black reality illustrates the kayfabe principle—everyone knows the performance is fake, but we keep applauding anyway.

FIREFLY FLASHPOINT

Hold on. Look around your workplace right now.
What expensive "innovation" is gathering dust?
What multi-million dollar transformation
changed only the vocabulary?
We all know the answer.
The question is: Why do we keep playing along?

STYLE OVER SUBSTANCE

WeWork's $47 billion valuation was built on the revolutionary idea of… renting desks. They called it "reimagining work," complete with kombucha on tap and meditation rooms, but strip away the performance, and you had commercial real estate with better marketing. While they burned through billions performing innovation, actual workplace transformation was happening quietly, with companies like Automattic and GitLab building fully distributed teams that questioned the very need for offices. The lesson? Real innovation often looks boring compared to "innovation theater." WeWork was an expensive production; the real revolution was happening on Slack channels and Zoom calls that no one thought to glamorize. The good news is that WeWork emerged from bankruptcy in May 2024. However, it's now valued significantly lower compared to its peak $47 billion valuation in January 2019.[23]

Or consider Theranos—$9 billion of pure performance art. Elizabeth Holmes didn't just fake blood tests; she faked an entire Silicon Valley narrative. Black turtlenecks channeling Steve Jobs. A board packed with luminaries who never asked to see the lab. Employees performing the charade of innovation while secretly sending samples to traditional labs. The real tragedy? While Theranos performed its theater, actual biotech companies were making genuine breakthroughs in diagnostics with far less fanfare. The media loved the drama of the young female founder disrupting the healthcare industry. They ignored the quiet labs doing real work because actual research makes for terrible magazine covers.

Juicero—the $400 Wi-Fi-connected juice press that venture capitalists funded with $120 million—epitomizes the reinvention racket. The performance was perfect: sleek design, Silicon Valley pedigree, subscriptions for proprietary juice packs. Then *Bloomberg* discovered you could squeeze the packs by hand faster than the machine could. The founder defended it as "more than a juice press"—it was a "platform." But platforms don't require $400 machines to squeeze $8 packets of precut fruit. While Juicero performed innovation, actual food entrepreneurs were building vertical farms and solving food deserts with zero fanfare and fractional funding.

There's a sadness, a shamelessness to these companies, but also, they are lost—they don't know how to respond to the chaos. HR departments and the corporate training industry spend $366 billion annually on programs that change nothing while firing employees who actually innovate. Many HR departments aren't developing talent—they're running protection rackets for mediocrity.

That's not just incompetence—that's systematic wealth extraction disguised as professional development because no one knows what to do next.

And it gets worse. HR departments are about to be buried alive under AI-generated resumes—thousands of perfectly crafted applications from candidates who may not even exist (in the sense of their resume). While they scramble to detect fake AI, actual talent is building companies that make HR departments irrelevant.

What flows downstream? Hiring freezes while companies "figure out" AI screening. Talented people are locked out by algorithmic gatekeepers. Entry-level positions requiring "AI detection expertise" that doesn't exist. Meanwhile, the builders bypass the whole broken system—they create value first, get noticed second, and get hired by people who recognize results over resumes.

WHEN PRETENSE BECOMES DANGEROUS

Back in those buried halls of the Domus Aurea, I thought about how medieval Romans, breaking through into these spaces, believed they'd found caves—*"grotte"* in Italian, from which we get the English word "grotesque." The beautiful became strange simply because it was out of context. The elaborate frescoes, humans merging with plants, mythical creatures in surreal patterns, once part of grand imperial spaces, now felt uncanny in their underground setting.

The same is now true for standardized tests measuring intelligence, keynote speakers selling transformation in hotel ballrooms, smartboards in classrooms where teachers buy supplies with their own salaries, and meditation pods in offices where no one has time to meditate.

The performance isn't just ineffective—it's actively harmful. Every failed revolution, every broken promise, every moment we choose performance over progress, we create more cynicism, more disengagement, more learned helplessness.

There's a species of firefly in which the female mimics the glow pattern of another species to lure unsuspecting males, not for mating, but for eating. The false glow proves fatal. Our institutional false glows—the pretense of innovation without substance, the rhetoric of transformation without change—are consuming our potential just as surely.

> **FIELD NOTES:** Some Photuris females can mimic up to 11 different species' flash patterns—they're like the ultimate corporate consultants of the firefly world.

THE GREAT UNMASKING

We're living through a moment of collective awakening. Like that medieval excavator crashing through Nero's ceiling, we've broken through the surface of our institutions and discovered the elaborate emptiness beneath. The performances that sustained generations—the rituals we inherited and never questioned—suddenly look as strange as those underground frescoes must have seemed by torchlight.

The pandemic didn't create this revelation; it simply accelerated it.

When the normal patterns broke, when we were forced to stop and actually look at what we were doing, the absurdity became undeniable. We became that wrestler who accidentally bleeds real blood in a fake fight—suddenly, the whole arena knows something authentic has pierced through the performance.

Across every sector, people are doing something unprecedented: They're walking away from the show.

The pandemic ripped away many veils.

When learning moved online, parents saw what actually happened in classrooms. When work went remote, the pointlessness of many office rituals became undeniable. We couldn't unsee what we'd seen.

Yet, even now, many institutions continue to double down on the performance. They add more buzzwords, more initiatives, more promises of transformation, while changing nothing fundamental. They mistake motion for progress, activity for achievement, and rhetoric for reality.

The Doubling Down Phenomenon. When institutions sense their kayfabe failing, they don't simplify—they amplify. Schools caught teaching obsolete curricula add "innovation labs." Companies exposed for meaningless metrics create more elaborate dashboards. It's pure panic disguised as progress. Like a comedian bombing on stage who talks faster and louder instead of trying new material, they mistake volume for value. The exposed magician doesn't learn new tricks; he just waves his hands more frantically, hoping motion will restore the illusion.

The Sunken Cost of Pretense. Imagine admitting that your hundred-million-dollar campus, your elaborate accreditation system, your entire organizational chart—all of it—serves no real purpose. The psychological weight would crush most leaders, so they don't admit it. Universities have spent centuries building credentialing monopolies. Corporations have constructed glass towers as monuments to hierarchy. To acknowledge the emptiness wouldn't just require change; it would invalidate their entire existence. Better to pretend the emperor's clothes are magnificent than face bankruptcy, both financial and spiritual.

A Nostalgia Trap. "Back in my day, a firm handshake and a strong work ethic ..." We've all heard it. This defense of broken systems isn't really about the systems—it's about mourning a past that exists only in memory's soft focus. The people who think this way are not defending actual education or actual work; they're defending their youth, their struggles, their stories of "making it." The four-year degree, the forty-year career, the gold watch—these aren't valued for what they produce but for what they represent: a world that made sense, where the rules were clear, where the performance at least promised a reliable ending. That world never existed, but try telling that to someone whose identity depends on it.

We've reached the point in the wrestling match where someone's mask has been torn off, revealing not a fearsome warrior but a tired actor underneath. And once you've seen the face behind the performance, you can never quite believe in the character again.

MOVING BEYOND PERFORMANCE

Standing in Nero's buried palace, I understood something crucial. The artists who later explored these ruins—Raphael sketching by candlelight, Renaissance minds learning from imperial excess—didn't come to replicate Nero's pretensions. They came to understand how beauty persists even when built on lies and confusing narratives, how truth eventually surfaces through centuries of rubble.

They transformed a monument to ego into a classroom for humility.

Real progress requires admitting that the performance has failed.

It means identifying where we're complicit in our own kayfabe—those comfortable lies we tell ourselves because confronting the truth seems too hard. Where in your life are you playing along with illusions to keep the peace, to keep things simple, and to keep the show going?

Progress happens not through better performances but through authentic engagement with messy reality. When ChatGPT exploded onto the scene, it succeeded not through elaborate promises but due to its radical simplicity.

No buzzwords. No hype. Just a text box that actually delivered what decades of "educational technology" had promised but never achieved.

THE CHOICE BEFORE US

We stand at a crossroads. We can continue the elaborate performances—adding more technology to broken systems, more metrics to measure meaningless outcomes, more rhetoric to mask inaction. Or we can do what those Renaissance artists did in Nero's ruins: Learn from the buried pretense and create something real.

This isn't about tearing everything down. Some traditions serve genuine purposes. But we must distinguish between customs that create value and performances that merely simulate it. The firefly's authentic glow serves a biological purpose—communication, mating, and survival. The false glow serves only deception and consumption.

Moving from performance to progress means embracing discomfort, abandoning rigid scripts, and allowing ourselves to write new narratives. It means being not just "future-ready" but "present-honest." The kayfabe affecting us right now demands confrontation before we can build anything meaningful.

Every generation builds its palaces of pretense. But truth, like those Renaissance artists discovered, has a way of surfacing through the rubble. The question is, will we continue to perform, or will we finally start progressing?

Here's an expanded, clearer version of this quirky firefly fact: nature gets darkly comedic and eerily relevant to our institutional pretenses.

Most fireflies use their glow for romance, flashing specific patterns like luminous love letters to attract mates. But some female fireflies have evolved a sinister trick. They've learned to mimic the flash patterns of other firefly species, sending out fake romantic signals to unsuspecting males from different groups.

Picture this: A hopeful male firefly sees what he thinks is the glow of his dreams. He flies over, expecting firefly romance. Instead, he becomes dinner.

The femme fatale firefly literally eats him.

She uses a false glow—a performance of attraction—to consume rather than create.

It's nature's perfect metaphor for institutional kayfabe. How many bright-eyed teachers answered the call of "innovative schools," only to be consumed by standardized testing? How many talented employees followed the glow of "dynamic workplaces," only to be devoured by soul-crushing bureaucracy? How many students chased the light of "transformative programs," only to emerge in debt and unprepared?

The authentic firefly glow—honest about what it is and what it offers—creates new life.

The false glow feeds on those who believe the performance. In nature, as in our institutions, the fake light doesn't just disappoint. It destroys.

So, when you see that next institutional glow—that promise of innovation, that pledge of transformation—ask yourself, "Is this the real flash of progress, or am I about to become someone's lunch?"

Choose your glow wisely.

REGENERATIVE MOMENT

Put down this book. Look around your current environment—office, home, school, wherever you are. Identify one piece of kayfabe, one performance everyone maintains despite knowing it's meaningless.

Maybe it's a meeting that accomplishes nothing. A report no one reads. A policy everyone ignores. A metric that measures nothing real.

Now ask yourself: *What would happen if someone simply ... stopped pretending? What if you were that someone?*

Sometimes the most radical act isn't adding something new but stopping something false. The Renaissance began not with new construction but with recognizing what lay buried beneath.

What pretense will you stop performing today? Remember, the quality of your learning will play an essential role in your future.

CHAPTER 3

THE TESTING SYNDROME & THE DEATH OF WONDER

"We are educating people out of their creative capacities."
— Sir Ken Robinson

Signal from the Future: *A fifth-grader listens to her mother's story of learning the food pyramid at school. Meanwhile, on her wrist, an AI band has already analyzed her genetic markers, current nutrient levels, and taste preferences to order tonight's dinner—perfectly calibrated for her growing body.*

It was supposed to be their moment of wonder. We'd just arrived in Tokyo after a grueling train ride from our base in Hiroshima, and the students of our traveling school were buzzing with anticipation. This was Tokyo—neon dreams, ancient temples, robot restaurants, a city where the future collides with tradition on every corner. It's the kind of place that makes you believe anything is possible, where vending machines sell everything from hot coffee to fresh eggs, where capsule hotels stack humans like friendly parcels, where ancient shrines sit quietly between glass towers reaching toward tomorrow.

I went looking for the grade-twelve students, expecting to find them planning their urban adventures, comparing subway maps, and debating whether to hit Harajuku or head straight for the Sky Tree. These kids had spent months traveling the world with us. They had studied rituals and worship in Hindu temples and the origins of a revolution in Boston, USA. Tokyo should have been their playground, their laboratory, their canvas.

Instead, I found them buried deep in textbooks in their rooms, with the curtains drawn against the city's electric glow. The familiar smell of highlighter pens and instant coffee filled the air. Practice papers lay scattered across the common areas, and the small desk lamps created streams of fluorescent anxiety in the gathering dusk.

"We can't," one of them said without looking up from her biology textbook. "Exams are in a couple of weeks."

There it was—the moment wonder died. Not dramatically, not with rebellion or tears. Just a quiet surrender. These brilliant young minds, transported to one of the world's most fascinating cities, were choosing standardized test prep over lived experience. The city that had inspired *Blade Runner* and *Ghost in the Shell*, that had rebuilt itself from rubble and raced into the future, couldn't compete with scoring rubrics.

There it was—the moment I understood the real crime.

Universities charge over $300,000 for degrees that teach skills that YouTube provides for free. We're not creating educated citizens—we're manufacturing debt slaves with fancy certificates, many of whom are potentially heading into financial servitude.

I felt guilty even suggesting it: "The Tokyo Tower is lit up, and it's lively out there. We could grab some ramen and walk around the local area."

They exchanged glances—that particular look of students who've learned to manage adult expectations while protecting their survival within the system we've created.

"Maybe tomorrow," another offered.

That night in Tokyo awakened something in me—a recognition that we don't just have antiquated systems. We've become professionals at extinguishing the human spark. We've industrialized the demise of curiosity into a dystopian nightmare. These students weren't wrong.

The system had trained them well.

Those test scores would determine their university options, their future trajectories, and their parents' pride. Tokyo would wait. Wonder could wait. The tests would not.

The assessment industrial complex profits from measuring what doesn't matter.

THE ARCHITECTURE OF CONFORMITY

For a long time, I pondered the events in Tokyo, unable to shake the image of those students trapped in their rooms while the city pulsed outside.

School after school presented the same façade—concrete boxes designed for control, not creativity. Through windows, I could see the familiar rows: It hits a little harder in Japan, whose schools often seem a little more gray than in other cities I've visited.

It reminded me of something I'd recently discovered about innovative architectural thinking. Japanese architect Takaharu Tezuka understood what we'd forgotten when he designed Tokyo's Fuji Kindergarten—a revolutionary circular building with no walls between classrooms, where children can run endless laps on the roof and trees grow through the structure itself. The building breathes. Children flow between spaces like water finding its level.

"My point is don't control them, don't protect them too much, and they need to tumble sometimes," Tezuka explained in his TED talk.

"They need to get some injury. And that makes them learn how to live in this world."[24] The kindergarten has no corners to hide in, no dead ends to get stuck in. The results are astounding: the average child at Fuji runs four thousand meters a day, and one particularly active boy was tracked running six thousand meters in a single morning.

To watch Takaharu Tezuka's Ted Talk, scan the QR code:

Movement breeds thinking. Collision creates innovation.

However, most of us don't learn or work in Tezuka's open circles. We exist in grids designed to prevent the very collisions that spark innovation. Walk into any traditional classroom, office, or examination hall and notice the design—rows of separated desks, individual cubicles, isolated workstations. The architecture itself declares war on wonder. There is no collision of ideas at the water cooler because it has been removed to increase "productivity." There is no spontaneous collaboration in open spaces because there are none.

Just human beings in boxes, producing standardized outputs.

I think of the stories from companies that broke this mold. When Steve Jobs designed Pixar's headquarters, he put the bathrooms in the center of the building (the atrium), forcing different departments to collide. Those collisions may have contributed to the creation of *Toy Story*, *Finding Nemo*, and *The Incredibles*. When Google designed its offices, it created micro-kitchens every 150 feet, ensuring no employee was ever more than a two-minute walk from a potential serendipitous encounter.

But these are exceptions. Most of us learn and work in structures designed during the industrial age for industrial purposes.

We've confused order with productivity, silence with learning, and separation with efficiency.

The typical work cubicle—that universal symbol of modern work—was invented in 1967 by Robert Propst,[25] who later called his creation "monolithic insanity" when he saw how companies implemented it. Even the inventor knew we were building cages for human potential. Propst came to despise his own creation.

WHEN CURIOSITY BECOMES DANGEROUS

I need you to pause here.

Think back—when was your wonder nearly extinguished?

What led to that moment? Was it systemic—a test that reduced your passion to a letter grade? Was it personal—someone who told you to stop asking so many questions? How long did it take to recover? Have you recovered?

Young children ask dozens of questions every hour, with preschoolers averaging over one hundred questions during active conversation.[26] By middle school, that number plummets to almost zero in classroom settings.[27] This isn't natural development—it's learned suppression. We train it out of them one "that's not on the test" at a time.

A five-year-old asks, "Why is the sky blue?" "How do airplanes stay up?" "Where do thoughts come from?" By fifteen, they've learned the only questions that matter are: "Will this be on the exam?" "What's the minimum score I need?" "How many pages should the essay be?"

We've replaced wonder with worry, curiosity with compliance.

FIREFLY FLASHPOINT

Which is the real dysfunction—the child or the system?

THE LANGUAGE OF CONTROL

George Orwell understood that controlling language means controlling thought. In *1984*, Newspeak doesn't just limit expression—it makes certain thoughts literally unthinkable. We've created our own educational Newspeak, drowning genuine learning in empty jargon.

"Learning journeys." "Growth mindsets." twenty-first-century skills." "Student-centered pedagogy." These beautiful words mask ugly realities. I visited an international school that prided itself on fostering "learning journeys." What did I see? Rote memorization. Teaching to the test. Students so focused on scores that they'd forgotten why they were learning.

The principal told me, "The teachers started well. They took risks and implemented dynamic projects, but as soon as accreditation and inspection were on the horizon, it all fell apart."

We use language to hide what we've done. We talk about "accountability" when we mean "control." We say "standards" when we mean "standardization." We promise "critical thinking" while penalizing anyone who thinks critically about the system itself.

IMAGINE A *PORTFOLIO* REVOLUTION

But alternatives exist. They've always existed. In the traveling school, born out of frustration with traditional models, the team worked toward completely abandoning standardized testing. Instead of cramming for exams, students curate portfolios of their learning journeys—real journeys, not the linguistic fabrication.

The shift wasn't easy. Parents panicked: "How will universities evaluate them?" Accreditation bodies resisted: "How do we measure standards?" Even some students, conditioned to the comfort of clear metrics, felt uneasy: "How do I know if I'm doing well?"

But then magic happened. Freed from test prep, students began following their curiosity.

I've traveled the world analyzing the impact of project-driven education and how releasing young people from a cycle of testing can unleash limitless potential. I've seen students, fascinated by water scarcity after visiting drought-stricken regions, design low-cost purification systems. One student said she didn't do it for a grade. She did it because she couldn't stop thinking about the children she had met who explained how they had faced challenges so alien it was hard to believe they were not talking about being raised in different periods of history. In light of such reflections, her portfolio included prototypes, failed experiments, community feedback, and implementation plans. No multiple-choice test could have captured that learning.

Imagine this applied to the business world, relating to the forever problem of performance reviews and encouraging authentic progression. Instead of relying on annual performance reviews and KPIs that incentivize short-term thinking, companies could evaluate employees through dynamic portfolios showcasing real impact: failed experiments that led to breakthroughs, cross-functional collaborations, and innovative solutions to actual business challenges. This shift would free professionals from "performing for metrics" and redirect their energy toward genuine problem-solving and value creation, much like those students who designed water purification systems not for grades, but because they couldn't stop thinking about the real people they wanted to help.

The urgency becomes clear when we look at what happens when professions lose their sense of purpose. Fifty years of data from teaching shows that increased standardization and top-down management—treating professionals like interchangeable parts—leads to a systematic decline in occupational prestige, talent attraction, and job satisfaction. The business world faces the same choice: continue measuring knowledge workers like factory workers, or embrace portfolio-based evaluation that celebrates intelligent failure and trusts professionals to navigate complexity.

The irony is that businesses already understand this with customers—authentic engagement beats manufactured metrics every time. It's time to apply that same wisdom to the people who create that customer value in the first place.

When we embraced portfolio-based assessment, the results were extraordinary. One student created a movie trailer for his book, contrasting colonial and post-colonial India—to this day, the only one I've ever seen. Another built an app connecting local artisans we'd met with global markets. She taught herself coding, studied international commerce, and wrestled with ethical questions about globalization. Her portfolio became a living document of problems encountered, solutions attempted, and lessons learned.

These weren't assignments. They were passionate responses to real-world encounters. The learning was deep, retained, and applicable. More importantly, it sustained rather than extinguished the students' wonder.

The skeptics always ask, "But how do you measure that? How do you ensure accountability?" As if a three-hour exam could capture the depth of learning that happens when wonder is unleashed. As if standardization ever produced innovation. As if the greatest minds in history succeeded because they scored well on standardized tests.

THE CORPORATE TESTING SYNDROME

This isn't limited to schools. The same soul-crushing logic has infected the corporate world. Performance reviews operate on identical principles: reducing human complexity to metrics, rating creativity on a five-point scale, and measuring innovation through standardized forms.

I know executives who spend more time preparing for performance reviews than actually performing. The review becomes the work. The measurement becomes the goal. PowerPoint presentations replace actual power. KPI dashboards substitute for key performance. Everyone knows it's theater but the show goes on.

A friend who works at a major consulting firm told me about their annual review process: "I spend three weeks writing self-assessments that no one reads, gathering 360-degree feedback that confirms what everyone already knows, and creating development plans I'll never follow. Then my manager, who's spent maybe ten hours with me all year, rates my 'innovation' on a scale of one to five. How do you quantify innovation? How do you standardize creativity?"

Meanwhile, companies that abandon traditional reviews report remarkable results. Netflix eliminated formal reviews in favor of continuous feedback. Adobe dropped annual reviews and saw voluntary turnover drop 30%. Deloitte restructured its entire approach after calculating that it spent two million hours a year on reviews that added no value.[28]

When you stop testing people, they start creating. When you remove the performance measurements, actual performance improves. However, most organizations, like most schools, cling to measurement theater because admitting its worthlessness would require confronting deeper questions about purpose, value, and trust.

FIREFLY FLASHPOINT

Your performance review measured your efficiency on a five-point scale. On that same scale, how would it rate your courage, your kindness, or your curiosity? Which list matters more?

CRUEL MATHEMATICS

The research is unequivocal. Neuroscientist Jaak Panksepp discovered that the brain's seeking system—what drives curiosity and exploration—is one of our primary emotional systems, as fundamental as fear or rage. When activated, it floods us with enthusiasm, energy, and joy. When suppressed, we experience what he called "psychic pain"—a profound discomfort that manifests as anxiety, depression, and disengagement.[29]

Author, speaker, and education advisor, the late Ken Robinson's famous TED talk—the most watched in history—resonated because it named what millions felt about eliminating creative capacities and the fact that "We're now running national education systems where mistakes are the worst thing you can make."[30]

To watch Ken Robinson's Ted Talk, scan the QR code:

However, knowing this changes nothing if we don't act. We've known about the damage of standardized testing for decades. Study after study shows it narrows curriculum, increases anxiety, discriminates against diverse learners, and fails to predict success in life, yet we double down, adding more tests, more metrics, more surveillance.

Why? Because testing isn't about learning. It's about sorting. It's about maintaining hierarchies. It's about creating the illusion of meritocracy while perpetuating existing power structures. The system isn't broken—it's working exactly as designed. That's the most terrifying realization of all.

Consider who benefits from the current system. The testing industry generates billions of dollars annually. These aren't educational institutions; they're businesses whose growth depends on more testing, not better learning. They lobby governments, fund research that supports their products, and create artificial scarcity through test dates and fees that privilege those who can afford multiple attempts.

But the machinery runs deeper. Standardized testing creates a beautiful fiction: that success is objective, measurable, and fair. It allows those who succeed to believe that they earned their position through merit alone, while those who fail internalize their "inadequacy." The child who tests poorly believes they're not smart. The employee who doesn't metric well believes they're not valuable. The system whispers, "This is your fault, not ours."

Meanwhile, test prep has become an industry of its own—it generates billions annually. Wealthy families hire tutors, buy practice tests, and send children to specialized camps. The poor make do with outdated prep books from the library, if they're lucky. Then we pretend the results measure ability rather than access. The gap widens, the hierarchy calcifies, and we call it meritocracy.

Even more insidious: Testing shapes consciousness itself. When everything is measurable, only the measurable matters. Kindness doesn't test well. Creativity resists standardization. Wisdom can't be bubbled in. So, we stop valuing what we can't measure, and soon, we stop seeing it at all. The child who comforts classmates, who asks unusual questions, who sees connections others miss—they learn that they're failing because their gifts don't fit the grid.

Teachers know this. In private conversations, away from administrators and parents, they'll tell you, "I became a teacher to inspire, to ignite curiosity. Now I'm a test prep coach. I teach strategies for eliminating wrong answers instead of seeking the truth. I watch brilliant children fit the mold, and I'm required to help them do it."

The sorting mechanism extends beyond school. Corporate hiring relies on the same logic—GPAs, test scores, credentials from "good" schools. Never mind that Google found no correlation between hiring metrics and job performance. In a 2013 interview with Thomas Friedman, Laszlo Bock, former VP of People Operations, stated that Google found

"GPAs are worthless as a criteria for hiring, and test scores are worthless ... We found that they don't predict anything."[31]

He elaborated that the proportion of people without any college education at Google had increased over time and that for many roles, academic performance showed no correlation with job performance. Never mind that some of our greatest innovators were terrible test-takers. The sorting must continue because the alternative—actually evaluating human complexity—is messy, subjective, and uncomfortable.

Here's the cruel mathematics of the system we've built instead: A stark report from the research firm Gartner reveals that 70% of employees feel they lack the skills to do their jobs well, yet only 25% believe their training was effective. Gartner calculates the cost of this broken system at a staggering $13.5 million per year for every one thousand employees.[32] We're not just failing—we're failing expensively.

Google's Project Oxygen conducted internal studies, analyzing their own hiring and performance data. They found that among the attributes that actually predicted success at Google, academic credentials and test scores ranked very low.[33]

And here's the darkest perspective: Those who succeed in this system often become its fiercest defenders. Having sacrificed their curiosity on the altar of achievement, they need to believe the sacrifice meant something. The executive who spent their youth cramming for tests can't admit it was meaningless—that would invalidate their entire journey. So, they impose the same system on the next generation. The abused become abusers, not from malice but from the need to justify their own pain.

This is how systems perpetuate themselves—through the conquered who become conquistadors, the tested who become testers, the sorted who become sorters. Each generation passes the trauma forward, calling it tradition, calling it standards, calling it preparation for the "real world"—as if the real world isn't desperate for exactly the qualities we're testing out of existence.

OPTIMIZING FOR MISERY

The devastating endgame of the testing syndrome is on stark display in China, where the national Gaokao exam is a high-pressure, all-or-nothing event that largely determines a student's future.[34] The entire country holds its breath. On exam days, traffic is diverted from test centers while police patrol the streets, silencing noisy neighbors. Outside the schools, nervous crowds of parents maintain a collective vigil, some burning incense to pray for their children's success. Yet the system they revere was famously bypassed by many of the nation's most celebrated entrepreneurs. Billionaire Jack Ma, founder of the e-commerce giant Alibaba, failed the Gaokao twice, proving that the rigid intelligence it measures is not the only kind that can change the world.

India's coaching centers prepare hundreds of thousands of teenagers for ultra-competitive engineering entrance exams. In cities dedicated to test preparation, childhood becomes an endless cycle of formula memorization and practice tests. Meanwhile, India's thriving startup ecosystem often emerges from those who chose different paths entirely.

But alternatives are flourishing. India's Atal Tinkering Labs[35] bring hands-on making and design thinking to millions of students. Hakuba International School in the stunning mountains of Nagano, Japan, focuses on helping young people and the planet flourish.[36] The Dalton School in Hong Kong has made tremendous strides with its innovative "Trailblazer" curriculum.[37] These programs measure success differently—through creativity sparked, problems solved, and curiosity sustained.

The pattern reveals itself: Systems optimized for test scores create exhausted, compliant students. Systems optimized for curiosity and human flourishing create engaged, innovative thinkers.

FORGOTTEN WONDER

When wonder dies, more than creativity is lost. We lose the capacity to imagine different futures, to question existing systems, to believe change is possible. A population trained in compliance won't challenge injustice. Workers who've never wondered won't innovate. Citizens who can't imagine alternatives won't create them.

I think of those students in Tokyo, and I see a generation being prepared for a world that no longer exists. They're studying for tests that AI can now pass perfectly. They're memorizing information that's instantly accessible. They're developing skills that automation will replace. Meanwhile, the one thing machines can't do—wonder, create, imagine, empathize—we're systematically training out of them.

Kill curiosity in childhood, and you've created adults who'll never ask dangerous questions. Make people afraid to be wrong, and they'll never risk being right about something new.

But here's the hope: Wonder is resilient. Even after decades of suppression, it can reignite. I've interviewed sixty-year-old executives who rediscover curiosity in design thinking workshops and become emotional as they realize what they've lost and found again. I've watched parents learning alongside their children in homeschool cooperatives, amazed at questions they'd forgotten how to ask. I've witnessed entire organizations transform when testing gives way to experimentation.

REKINDLING THE FLAME

The firefly that stops glowing doesn't immediately die—it enters dormancy. Given the right conditions, it can illuminate again. The same is true for human wonder, but it requires intention, courage, and often a willingness to break rules.

Some companies now build "wonder time" into workweeks—Google's famous "20% time," which produced Gmail and AdSense.

However, Yahoo CEO Marissa Mayer once said that this 20% time was really 120% time, done in addition to regular work.[38] Schools experiment with "genius hour," where students pursue passion projects. What I found in my own research was that *genius hour* was often squeezed between test prep and the standard curriculum.

These are often temporary fixes for a broken system. Real change requires deeper transformation. What if we designed spaces for collision, not isolation? What if we measured growth through portfolios, not percentages? What if we valued questions more than answers?

I think of educators like Sugata Mitra, who put computers in slums and watched children teach themselves. His "hole in the wall" New Delhi experiment proved that curiosity is more powerful than curriculum.[39] Or think of the innovation powerhouse 3M. Their famous "15% Rule" gave engineers the freedom to chase their own curiosity on company time.[40] That single policy didn't just create the Post-it Note; it built an empire on serendipity.

However, individual examples aren't enough. We need systemic change, and that begins with each of us refusing to let our wonder die.

THE UNSCHOOLING OF CONSCIOUSNESS

Can you unlearn the learned helplessness of standardized systems? Can you reprogram yourself after decades of conditioning? The answer is yes, but it requires conscious effort.

Start with language. Notice when you use education-speak or corporate jargon. Replace "learning outcomes" with "what fascinates me." Swap "performance metrics" for "meaningful impact." Language shapes thought—change your words, change your mind.

Practice productive confusion. When you encounter something new, resist the urge to immediately use Google or AI to find the answer. Sit with not knowing. Let questions marinate. Wonder thrives in the space between curiosity and resolution.

Seek environments that encourage intellectual risk. Join communities where "I don't know" is a beginning, not an ending. Surround yourself with people who ask, "What if?" more than, "What's the right answer?"

THE CHOICE BEFORE US

We stand at an inflection point. Artificial intelligence can now pass any standardized test we devise. Students can generate perfect essays in seconds. The testing industrial complex is collapsing under its own obsolescence.

This crisis is an opportunity. We can double down on surveillance, create more elaborate ways to ensure "academic integrity," and build higher walls around crumbling systems. Or we can admit what we've always known: Standardized testing measures compliance, not capability.

The students in Tokyo chose test prep over discovery because we built a system that punishes wonder. But that system is dying. The question is: What will we build in its place?

The firefly's glow serves a biological purpose—communication, mating, and survival. When we dim that light early, we don't just lose beauty; we lose the next generation's capacity to illuminate new paths forward.

CLOSE THIS BOOK.

Find a piece of paper—yes, actual paper. The physical act of writing by hand activates different neural pathways than typing. Set a timer for five minutes.

Now write down three questions that fascinated you as a child but that you stopped asking. Maybe "Why do we dream?" "What happens after we die?" "Why do people hurt each other?" or "Could animals talk if we taught them?" Don't Google them. Don't seek answers. Just let the questions exist.

Feel the discomfort of not knowing. Notice the urge to immediately find answers. That discomfort is your wonder trying to reawaken, pushing against years of conditioning that taught you that not knowing equals failure.

Next, identify three practices you could build into your daily life to keep curiosity alive:

- Could you take a different route to work each day, noticing one new detail?
- Could you have lunch monthly with someone from a completely different field?
- Could you spend one hour weekly exploring a subject you know nothing about?
- Could you keep a "wonder journal" of questions without immediately seeking answers?
- Could you practice saying, "I don't know," without shame or apology?
- Could you ask, "Why?" five times about something you take for granted?

Finally, make one commitment: This week, ask a question you're afraid sounds stupid. Ask it in a meeting. Ask a friend. Ask yourself. Notice what happens—not just the answer you receive, but how it feels to wonder aloud again.

The five-year-old you is still in there, bursting with questions about airplanes, vegetables, and monsters under the bed. That child doesn't need education.

That child needs permission.

Grant it.

Before you do, remember: Every great discovery began with someone willing to look foolish. Every innovation started with someone saying,

"I wonder what would happen if…" Every breakthrough emerged from someone refusing to accept "because that's how it's always been done."

Your wonder isn't childish. It's revolutionary.

Light it up.

ARC TWO
IGNITING SPARKS: BUILDING THE NEW LEARNING & LEADERSHIP PARADIGM

"A candle loses nothing by lighting another candle."
— James Keller

The old lights are dimming. We've seen that clearly enough—the collapse of time-based hierarchies, the great pretense of institutional performance, the systematic demise of wonder in our schools and workplaces. We could spend more chapters cataloging the darkness, adding to the literature of decline, but that's not why you're here, and it's not why I'm writing.

Something else is happening. Right now, as you read these words, new lights are beginning to flash.

Around the world, in classrooms and boardrooms, in startups and ancient communities, a different kind of learning is emerging. Not the heavy, hierarchical systems of the past—those industrial monuments to control and conformity—but something lighter, faster, more alive. Something that glows from within rather than waiting for external illumination.

I call it "firefly learning." The "firefly mindset." *The firefly effect.* Once you see it, you can't unsee it—these brief, brilliant flashes of authentic transformation happening everywhere the old systems are weakening.

It's happening in companies like Netflix and Spotify, which have replaced command-and-control hierarchies with context and collaboration. Netflix's famous culture deck doesn't talk about rules and compliance—it talks about freedom and responsibility. Spotify's agile squads self-organize around problems that matter. Both companies move at firefly speed, iterating and innovating while their competitors cling to five-year plans.

It's happening where indigenous communities use cutting-edge AI to preserve ancestral wisdom. In New Zealand, the Māori-led broadcaster Te Hiku Media built its own platform, Whare Kōrero ("house of speech"), to avoid ceding control to global tech giants. The platform holds over thirty years of digitized archives—a thousand hours of native speakers, some born in the late nineteenth century. To make this treasure accessible, they used NVIDIA's open-source tools to build a speech recognition model that now transcribes their language with 92% accuracy.[41] It's a stunning example of ancient knowledge meeting modern technology, with neither diminishing the other.

Most importantly, it's happening inside people who've stopped waiting for permission to learn, to lead, to light up their small corner of the world. The homeschooling parent who realizes they don't need a teaching degree to ignite their child's curiosity. The employee who starts a learning circle at work without asking HR's permission. The retiree who teaches coding to kids in their community and discovers that they're learning as much as they're teaching.

These aren't isolated incidents. They're signals of a profound shift—from heavy to light, from external to internal, from controlled to emergent. The firefly doesn't wait for instructions on when to glow. It generates its own light in response to conditions, creating patterns of communication and connection that no central authority could design.

WHAT YOU'LL DISCOVER

In the next three chapters, we'll explore this new paradigm together, not as distant observers analyzing a trend, but as participants ready to generate our own light.

Chapter 4: The Firefly Mindset reveals how to generate your own illumination instead of waiting for external validation. We'll discover why artificial intelligence makes human curiosity more valuable than ever, not less. I'll share the six elements that create regenerative learning cycles, patterns I've observed in every authentic transformation I've witnessed. You'll learn why some people thrive in uncertainty while others cling to dying systems, and more importantly, you'll learn how to become one of the thrivers.

Chapter 5: The Reinvention Racket exposes the difference between fake innovation and authentic transformation. We'll learn to spot expensive theater—those million-dollar "digital transformations" that change nothing but the vocabulary. Why do most AI solutions fail? Why do innovation labs produce so little innovation? How can you tell when an organization has stopped pretending and started progressing? I'll share stories from the front lines of both real and fake change, giving you a decoder ring for distinguishing glitter from genuine glow.

Chapter 6: Holding On and Letting Go navigates the delicate balance between ancient wisdom and cutting-edge tools. What should we preserve from thousands of years of human learning? What must we release to embrace what's emerging? We'll explore why the most powerful transformations happen when timeless principles guide new technology, not when we abandon the past or blindly worship the future. This is about integration, not replacement—using AI to amplify human wisdom, not substitute for it.

FROM THEORY TO IGNITION

This isn't about theory. I've read enough books that analyze problems without offering solutions, that describe the darkness without showing how to generate light. This is about ignition—the moment when understanding transforms into action, when knowledge becomes capability, when you stop waiting for someone else to fix the system and start creating alternatives.

By the end of these three chapters, you won't just understand firefly thinking—you'll be living it. You won't just recognize authentic innovation—you'll be creating it. You won't just appreciate the balance between old and new—you'll embody it.

Here's what I've learned after years of watching systems fail and new approaches emerge: The world doesn't need more people who can analyze problems. We have plenty of those, thank you, writing reports about the darkness while sitting in it. Instead, the world needs people who can spark solutions. It doesn't need more followers of other people's frameworks—we're drowning in methodologies. It needs fireflies generating their own light, creating patterns of possibility that inspire others to glow.

The spark is already inside you. It's been there since you were five years old, asking why the sky was blue. It survived years of standardized tests, performance reviews, and institutional kayfabe. It's waiting, like a firefly in dormancy, for the right conditions to flash.

We can create those conditions together, not through another strategic plan, reorganization, or innovation initiative, but through something simpler and more profound—remembering how to generate our own light.

It starts with a single moment when everything changes. For me, that moment came in an unexpected place, at an unexpected time, and through an unexpected teacher. It changed how I see learning, leading, and living.

Let me show you how it can change things for you, too.

The old systems are dying. Good. Let them go, offering them gratitude for what they gave us. The new lights are already beginning to flash. The only question is: Will you be one of them?

Time to find out.

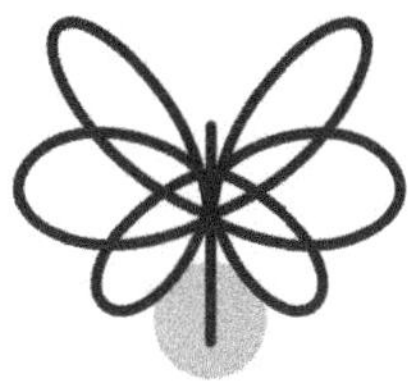

CHAPTER 4

THE FIREFLY MINDSET: REGENERATIVE, RESILIENT, REAL

"Be yourself; everyone else is already taken."
— Oscar Wilde

Signal from the Future: *During lunch, Mark reflects on this AI assistant handling his entire job for three months while he's been teaching pottery at the community center. His colleague Jasmine, still manually updating spreadsheets "to stay relevant," hasn't noticed. Mark debates whether to tell her or let her keep developing the growing friendship with his AI assistant, "Maya."*

THE NIGHT EVERYTHING CHANGED

Three years into teaching at the world's first traveling high school, I hit a wall. Not the inspiring kind you break through using motivational speeches from YouTube, but the soul-crushing kind that makes you question everything you thought you knew about education and why you do what you do.

As an educator I was situated at a cloud forest research station halfway up a mountain in Costa Rica, the kind of place where the humidity wraps around you like a second skin. Our students—brilliant, curious teenagers from around the world—had chosen this unconventional path because they hungered for something different. They wanted education that moved, that breathed, that connected to the real world in ways traditional schools couldn't offer.

That particular day, I'd just finished teaching yet another history lesson. It was February, which meant it was the Cold War and its proxy conflicts, the same content I'd delivered for years. My PowerPoint was polished enough to withstand the slew of questions that would follow. I knew where the confusion would arise and what every conceptual tripwire might be. I could teach this material in my sleep—and that was precisely the problem.

The electricity between teacher and material had died. Students had become performers in educational theater, dutifully taking notes they'd memorize for exams and forget by summer. I'd become another actor in the same tired production, delivering lines I'd rehearsed too many times. We were all just going through the motions, checking boxes on a curriculum designed by people who'd never met these particular humans with their particular gifts.

I left the classroom that day feeling hollow. Not like a failure, exactly, but like a fraud. Every teacher claims that they want to make a difference, ignite curiosity, and change lives, but there I was, extinguishing the very spark I'd claimed to nurture, making these brilliant young minds conform to a standardized curriculum instead of helping them create their own learning adventures.

That evening, I sat on the research station's patio with the other teachers, nursing a drink and my bruised idealism. As darkness fell, the fireflies emerged—hundreds of them, maybe thousands—transforming the forest into a living constellation. In the absence of television, the internet, or any other form of entertainment beyond books and conversation, watching these creatures became our nightly meditation.

The experience crystallized the idea that growth equals glow—it's not always about the destination; it's about how brightly you shine on the journey.

THE TEACHER IN THE TREES

At first, I watched the fireflies the way I'd been trained to observe most things—analytically, looking for patterns to explain, systems to understand. But something about that particular night, maybe the sting of my classroom failure, made me see things differently.

These creatures weren't performing for anyone. They weren't following a curriculum or meeting standards. They were generating their own light from within, each flash authentic and purposeful. When one lit up, it triggered others—not through hierarchy or command, but through some organic communication that spread through the entire forest like gossip at a small-town café.

Some flashed quickly, some slowly.

Some gathered in groups, pulsing together like a biological disco. Others remained solitary, adding their singular voice to the larger conversation. But every flash was real. They weren't caused by reflected light bouncing off something else. It wasn't external illumination that made them visible, but light generated from within, powered by their own chemical fire.

I sat there for hours, my cold drink growing warm in my hand, watching this natural light show. Slowly, a recognition dawned that would change everything about how I understood learning, leading, and living.

I realized that we'd been thinking about education completely backwards.

Traditional education asks, "How do we make them learn?" It assumes darkness as the default state and views the teacher's role as one of shining light on students, illuminating them from the outside. We create elaborate systems of external motivation, such as grades, gold stars, class rankings, and honor rolls. We build hierarchies where knowledge flows downward from those who know to those who don't.

But what if that's entirely wrong? What if every human being already carries their own light, and our job isn't to illuminate them but to create conditions where their inner light can emerge?

The fireflies had no teachers, no curriculum, no standardized tests, yet they'd mastered the art of illumination, creating patterns of communication and beauty that put our educational systems to shame. Each firefly generated its own light. That light triggered others to glow. Together, they created something magnificent that no central authority could have designed.

That night in Costa Rica, watching those self-powered "lightning bugs" paint the darkness with purpose, I realized that we needed an entirely different question, not "How do we make them learn?" but "How do we help them glow?"

Failure plus reflection equals flash—every dim moment prepares us for a brighter light.

THE BIRTH OF FIREFLY THINKING

Let me break down what I learned from my firefly teachers and how it's become even more crucial in our age of artificial intelligence.

Core Element One: Self-Powered Light

Every firefly generates its own light through a chemical reaction called bioluminescence. They don't need external power sources, validation, or someone else to flip their switch. The light comes from within, triggered by their own purposes—mating, warning, communicating.

Most of our educational and corporate systems are built on external motivation, including grades, promotions, performance reviews, and quarterly bonuses. We've created entire generations of people who can't learn without someone telling them what to learn, when to learn it, and whether they've learned it correctly. We've trained humans to be mirrors, reflecting light rather than generating it.

But here's what keeps me up at night in 2025: Artificial intelligence now outperforms humans on most standardized tests. ChatGPT can write better essays than the average college student. Claude can solve complex problems faster than most professionals.

As mentioned earlier in the book, a 2024 study published in Scientific Reports found that ChatGPT-4 outperformed college students on divergent thinking tasks—the standard measure of creative potential. The AI scored in the top 1% for originality and fluency compared to human responses.[42] Let that sink in. The machines are literally out-creating us on the very tests we designed to measure human creativity.

If our value as humans is based on performing well on standardized assessments, we've already lost. If our education system's goal is to produce people who can follow instructions and reproduce information, AI will do it better, faster, and cheaper. The external-light model of education is obsolete.

But here's the firefly insight that changes everything: AI can generate content, but it can't generate purpose. It can create patterns, but it can't feel the significance of discovery. It can process information about love, loss, triumph, and tragedy, but it can't experience the weight of those moments.

I think of standing with students at Hiroshima's Peace Memorial, feeling the weight of history in our bones. AI can tell you the facts—140,000 casualties, 8:15 a.m., August 6, 1945—but it can't feel the gut punch of seeing the dark shadows on the neighborhood walls that signify people's final moments. It also can't experience the collective silence of thirty teenagers suddenly understanding what humans are capable of as we conduct a deep dive into human ethics. Watch a group of students debate the trolley problem—that classic ethical dilemma of whether to let a runaway trolley kill five people or pull a lever to divert it, killing one instead. Once you see the intensity of young people grappling with these impossible choices, you'll never ignore the small philosophical moments again. That moment of recognition, that inner light of comprehension mixed with horror and hope—that's purely human.

The most powerful learning in the age of AI isn't human versus machine. It's human with machines, where your self-generated purpose guides technology's processing power and where your inner light illuminates what matters among the infinite information AI can provide.

Core Element Two: Chain Reaction Signaling

When one firefly lights up, it triggers others, not through command and control, but through authentic signaling that spreads organically through the forest. Real learning creates more learning. Genuine curiosity is contagious. Authentic passion spreads like wildfire—or like firefly light through a Costa Rican forest.

This is what's possible when there is an approach that allows for learning and enables us to follow our passions and interests. No teacher assigned this. No curriculum demanded it. One authentic spark of curiosity triggered a chain reaction of learning that went deeper than any textbook chapter ever could.

At the second annual Hakuba Forum, we discussed how researchers are using AI to analyze patterns in indigenous knowledge systems across multiple cultures. AI can process vast amounts of data, identifying similarities in agricultural practices, astronomical observations, and medicinal plants across continents, correlating information that would take human researchers decades to compile.

But here's what fascinated me: The AI couldn't tell the researchers which patterns mattered. It couldn't feel the sacred weight of a healing ceremony or understand why certain stars hold stories that bind communities together. It couldn't experience the taste of soil that tells an indigenous farmer when to plant or the change in wind that signals seasonal transition.

The human researchers' curiosity—their inner light—had to guide the AI's analysis. Their questions shaped what patterns emerged as significant. Their cultural understanding transformed data into wisdom. The chain reaction occurred not in the machine itself, but between humans who used the machine as a tool.

Compare this to most corporate training, where people sit through PowerPoint presentations and leave unchanged. There's no authentic spark, so there's no chain reaction. It's just individuals consuming content instead of communities creating knowledge together—a dead light that triggers nothing.

Core Element Three: Regenerative Cycles

Fireflies don't glow constantly. They flash intensely, then rest, then flash again—often brighter than before. This isn't laziness or inefficiency. The dark periods are when they build the chemical energy for the next burst of light.

We've built systems that demand constant performance. Students move from class to class, test to test, with little time to integrate their learning. Employees rush from meeting to meeting without space to think. We've confused constant motion with progress, forgetting that sustainable brilliance requires regeneration.

In our traveling school, we learned this the hard way. In the first years of our redesigned curriculum, after we reacted to the lessons of Costa

Rica, we crammed every moment with activities, classes, and cultural experiences. Both students and staff burned out. Learning became surface-level and performative—we were racing through experiences without integration.

So we simplified. We removed noise instead of adding complexity. This gave students space to pursue passion projects, tune into their natural rhythms, have meaningful conversations, or simply exist. The paradox: doing less led to learning more.

The results were transformative. Students who returned reacted to the simplicity with deeper insights, unexpected connections, and renewed energy. One student designed a smartwatch concept to detect suicide risk, monitoring physical symptoms like heart rate and stress levels, turning her concern about mental health statistics into a potentially life-saving innovation. Another explored Mayan culture through experiential art, transforming her time in Tulum during the pandemic into a creative piece that bridged ancient wisdom with contemporary expression. A third designed sustainable farming systems for urban environments, applying closed-system ecosystem principles learned from creating BioBottles to reimagine food production in cities.

The rest periods we designed into the system weren't empty—they were generative. Students weren't just processing information; they were creating solutions to real problems, from mental health crises to food security. Each project emerged from genuine concern married to creative application.

In the age of AI, this becomes even more critical. AI can work 24/7, processing constantly. But humans aren't machines—we're fireflies. We need cycles: flash and rest, engage and integrate, research and reflect.

The most effective learners I know embrace this rhythm. They use AI intensively for research and idea generation, then step away completely. During these pauses, their human intelligence processes what actually matters. Insight comes not from constant consumption but from knowing when to flash and when to go dark.

Core Element Four: Synchronicity over Hierarchy

Perhaps most importantly, fireflies synchronize through mutual influence, not top-down control. In certain species of fireflies, thousands of them will pulse in perfect unison, creating waves of light that can be seen for miles. No single firefly conducts this symphony. They achieve synchronicity through a responsive relationship, each adjusting to the other until harmony emerges.

> **FIELD NOTES:** The Great Smoky Mountains' synchronous fireflies (Photinus carolinus) flash in unison for just two weeks each year, drawing thousands of visitors to witness nature's own light show.

Traditional hierarchies assume that knowledge flows downward—from teacher to student, from manager to employee, from expert to novice. But in rapidly changing environments, the most valuable insights often come from the edges, from those closest to emerging problems and possibilities.

We learned this by organizing our education summit in Japan, the Hakuba Forum. Instead of bringing in outside experts to lecture, we required every participant—teacher, student, parent, administrator—to give a four-minute "frontier talk" about one edge they were pushing in their own learning or work. No slides, no status markers, just humans sharing what they were discovering at their personal frontiers.

The magic wasn't in any individual talk but in the collective intelligence that emerged. A sixteen-year-old's experiments with AI music composition inspired a sixty-year-old teacher to rethink assessment. A parent's struggle with work-life balance sparked insights about educational rhythms. Everyone taught, everyone learned, and rigid hierarchies dissolved into networks of mutual illumination.

This is what organizations that embrace firefly thinking create—networks where influence flows in all directions, where collective intelligence emerges from individual lights synchronizing not through control but through authentic response to each other.

THE FIREFLY FRAMEWORK

Over years of experimenting with these principles, a pattern emerged. I call it the "firefly framework"—six interconnected elements that create regenerative learning and leadership in any context and that are especially powerful in our AI-enhanced age.

Picture a **Firefly Wheel**, where each element flows into the next, creating sustainable cycles of growth and illumination:

1. **At Dusk (Foundation & Connection):** Begin by understanding your place within the system. Everything connects—your learning affects mine; my growth impacts ours. We dig deep to understand problems as part of living ecosystems, not isolated issues.

2. **Into the Dance (Build & Iterate):** From a strong foundation, we build. We experiment, fail, learn, rebuild. Every failure fuels the next attempt. Resilience isn't about avoiding challenges but about using them to shine brighter.

3. **As a Beacon (Share & Amplify):** What we build must be shared. Learning that stays with one person dies. We become bridges between ideas, people, and cultures. Our discoveries ripple outward, triggering others to glow.

4. **Toward Constellation (Imagine & Project):** Sharing leads to dreaming bigger. Not prediction but possibility. Not certainty but curiosity about what could emerge. We see patterns in what is and imagine what could be.

5. **In Harmony (Evaluate & Align):** Big visions require wise choices. With power comes responsibility. We must consider not only what we can do, but also what we should do. Ethics guide expansion.

6. **Until Dawn (Rest & Regenerate):** Sustainable learning requires rhythm. Intensity followed by integration. Effort followed by rest. We honor natural cycles, building energy for the next rotation.

Then back to dusk—but deeper, wiser, more connected ...

This isn't another framework to memorize or implement mechanically. It's a recognition that learning is a living system, not a mechanical process. Each element feeds the others. When you strengthen your roots in the community, your vision clarifies. When you develop resilience through iteration, your stories become more powerful. When you honor natural rhythms, your balance improves.

The Firefly Wheel

Six-Phase Regenerative Learning Cycle

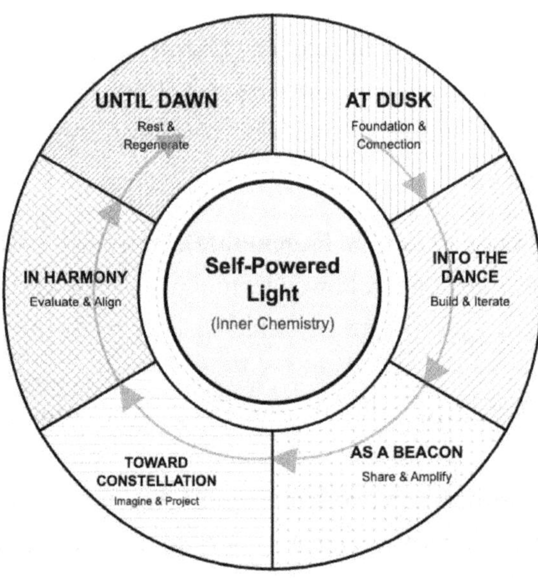

"Each element feeds the others. When you strengthen your roots, your vision clarifies."

Figure 3: The Firefly Wheel - Six-Phase Regenerative Learning Cycle. Unlike linear progression models, this framework mirrors nature's regenerative patterns. Each phase feeds the next: Foundation & Connection (At Dusk) → Build & Iterate (Into the Dance) → Share & Amplify (As a Beacon) → Imagine & Project (Toward Constellation) → Evaluate & Align (In Harmony) → Rest & Regenerate (Until Dawn). The cycle then deepens, with each rotation building on previous insights. Just as fireflies flash in patterns rather than glowing continuously, sustainable learning requires rhythms of intensity and integration.

THE "DIRTY PROTOTYPE" METHOD

Let me walk you through your first learning cycle with painful specificity because abstract frameworks don't create transformation—executed plans do. Choose your domain. Let's say Thursday. Not "sometime this week"—Thursday, 5:00 p.m., decision locked. Pick something that makes you nervous-excited, that sweet spot between terror and curiosity. For me, it was blockchain technology. I knew nothing about it and felt stupid asking questions—perfect. Your domain should make you feel similarly incompetent. If you're comfortable, you've chosen incorrectly.

Week One: Monday morning, create three AI accounts—Claude for deep analysis, Perplexity for research, and ChatGPT for brainstorming.

First prompt: "I know nothing about [your domain]. Create a two-week learning plan that takes me from complete ignorance to conversational competence. Include daily 30-minute exercises."

Follow the plan religiously.

When you feel like skipping because "life got busy," remember: You're training your learning muscles, not just acquiring information. Document everything in a simple Google Doc—questions that arise, connections to your existing knowledge, moments of confusion. The documentation matters more than the learning because it reveals your learning patterns.

By **Week Two**, start building something terrible. I built the world's worst blockchain course using one of these Canva-like apps—with awful images, stumbling explanations, and technical errors throughout—but creating it forced me to confront what I didn't understand.

Share your terrible creation with someone by Day 14.

The shame of public inadequacy accelerates learning faster than any course.

Week Three: Find three people actually working in your domain. LinkedIn makes this easy—message ten, and three will respond. Ask them one question: "What do beginners always get wrong?"

Their answers will reframe everything.

Week Four: Rebuild your terrible creation with new understanding. The improvement will shock you. This isn't about becoming an expert—it's about proving to your nervous system that you can learn anything in a set period of time.

Once you complete a cycle, you'll get comfortable with a concept we call "dirty prototyping."

What do I mean by the dirty or messy prototype? Dirty prototyping means building something gritty and unpolished in 48 hours rather than planning something perfect for days, because imperfect can be improved. IDEO famously redesigned the shopping cart in five days for ABC's Nightline using cardboard, zip ties, and bike parts—proving that rapid iteration beats endless planning.[43] This feature showcased IDEO's commitment to multidisciplinary team brainstorming, the research process, prototyping, and the importance of gathering user feedback. IDEO's shopping cart design evolved from an idea to a working appearance model in just four days.

FIREFLY FLASHPOINT

When did you last learn something without being told to?
If it's been more than a month, your light is already dimming.

EVIDENCE FROM THE FIELD

Let me show you what firefly thinking looks like when organizations actually embrace it, especially in our AI-enhanced world.

Netflix's Cultural Revolution

Netflix didn't become a streaming giant by improving its DVD delivery service. They asked a firefly question: "What if people could access any story, anytime, anywhere?" That self-powered curiosity led them to completely reimagine the entertainment industry.

But what most people miss is that their famous culture deck isn't about rules and procedures. It's pure firefly thinking—freedom and responsibility, context not control, high performance with high integrity. They hire people who can generate their own light, give them context and tools, and then let them illuminate their own path.

Yes, Netflix uses AI for content recommendations and production decisions, but human creativity drives their strategy. The algorithm can tell you what people watched; only humans can imagine what they might want to watch next that doesn't yet exist.

Spotify's Squad System

Historically, Spotify organizes into small, autonomous teams called squads—essentially firefly swarms. Each squad has a clear mission but complete freedom in execution. When one squad discovers something valuable, it spreads organically to others through guilds and tribes, not through top-down mandates.

They use AI extensively for personalization, music discovery, and now playlist generation. But human teams make creative decisions about product direction. Don't be surprised to see AI more heavily involved in advertisement choices and podcast translation in the near future. This means that the AI processes patterns; humans decide which patterns to amplify.

Finland's Education System

Finland transformed its education system not by standardizing more but by standardizing less. They embraced firefly principles before AI was even a factor. Short school days with long breaks. Professional autonomy for teachers. Learning through phenomena rather than subjects.

Now they're integrating AI not to replace teachers but to free them for what only humans can do—inspire, empathize, and create conditions for inner light to emerge. AI is beginning to handle administrative tasks and basic skill practice, giving teachers more time for the essentially human work of education.

Education Estonia

Estonia is taking firefly principles even further with AI Leap 2025. While other nations debate AI integration, Estonia is already providing 20,000 students and 3,000 teachers with comprehensive AI tools and training, building on their successful Tiger Leap digital transformation from the 1990s. Students use AI as creative partners to solve real community problems. Teachers become learning designers rather than information deliverers. The entire system operates on firefly logic: distributed innovation, self-directed discovery, and technology that amplifies human creativity rather than replacing it. Estonia isn't just teaching with AI—they're teaching a generation to glow brighter because of it.

YOUR PERSONAL FIREFLY MOMENT

Here's what strikes me most about our current moment: Three years ago, most of us knew nothing about AI. It wasn't in job descriptions, wasn't required expertise, and wasn't part of daily conversation. Now it's everywhere, transforming every domain of human activity.

Think about that. In less time than it takes to get an undergraduate degree, a technology emerged that challenges fundamental assumptions about human intelligence, creativity, and purpose. If you were following a five-year plan made in 2019, how relevant would it be now?

This is why firefly thinking matters more than ever. We can't predict what technologies or challenges will emerge in the next three years. We can't create curricula for jobs that don't yet exist. We can't plan for disruptions we can't imagine.

But we can cultivate the capacity to generate our own light. We can create conditions for authentic learning to spread. We can build resilience through regenerative cycles. We can synchronize without hierarchy.

Ask yourself: Where in your life are you waiting for someone else to turn on your light? What skill have you postponed learning because the "right" course hasn't appeared? What creative project sits dormant because you're not "ready"? What leadership challenge are you avoiding because you don't have permission?

What would self-powered learning look like in that area? Not waiting for perfect conditions but beginning with what you have? Using AI as a research assistant and thinking partner while keeping your human curiosity at the center? Giving yourself six months—not five years—to make significant progress?

Here's what I know from watching thousands of learners navigate this new landscape: The people who thrive won't be those who use AI most or those who avoid it entirely; they'll be those who generate their own light and use technology to amplify their authentic glow.

PARTNERS, NOT MASTERS

The transformation is already happening, faster than most realize. When BCG surveyed global organizations, they discovered something stunning: Two-thirds of people expect to use AI in education, health, and work within the next year. Not five years. Not "someday." Within twelve months.[44]

Yet here's the gap that creates opportunity—employees are adopting AI far faster than their leaders realize. While boardrooms debate policy, workers are quietly revolutionizing their daily tasks. They're not waiting for permission; they're creating the complementarity economy where the majority see AI as an augmentation rather than a replacement.

As education leader Darren Coxon beautifully describes it, "AI should walk beside us as a companion and behind us as support, but never in front of us as our leader." He calls this ideal relationship a "cybernetic classmate," emphasizing learning together rather than one teaching the other. Darren remains one of the finest practitioners at making even the most skeptical feel a degree of warmth towards AI; however, he warns that AI should not be allowed to lead us by the hand into the abyss: "The moment AI walks in front, we've surrendered our uniquely human capacity to choose direction, to wonder why we're walking at all, to decide when to pause and admire the view."

This aligns with Wharton professor Ethan Mollick's research on what he calls "co-intelligence." In his book of the same name, Mollick found that the most successful AI users don't treat it as either an oracle or a servant, but as a thinking partner. His concept of the "jagged frontier"—where AI excels at surprisingly complex tasks while failing at seemingly simple ones—reveals why human judgment remains irreplaceable. As he puts it, we need to "always invite AI to the table," but keep humans at the head of it.[45]

The momentum is also building across emerging economies. Bangladesh's vision for 2050 shows us what's possible when nations embrace transformation rather than resist it.[46] They're not just digitizing old processes—they're reimagining entire systems. With internet penetration at 38.9% and mobile subscribers exceeding 170 million, they're leapfrogging traditional development stages. Their digital economy aims to position Bangladesh among the top ten IT outsourcing hubs globally by 2050, while AI-driven solutions are being integrated across healthcare, agriculture, and manufacturing. This isn't about catching up to developed nations—it's about creating entirely new pathways that combine technological innovation with human creativity. The shift from following to leading is happening faster than traditional institutions can comprehend.

FIREFLY FLASHPOINT

When AI can do your job better, faster, and cheaper —what's left of you?

THE PATH FORWARD

The firefly mindset isn't complicated. Generate your own light. Let it trigger others. Honor regenerative cycles. Synchronize without hierarchy obsession. Most critically, use technology to amplify rather than replace your human essence. Never surrender that irreducible core of curiosity, empathy, and creative mischief that no algorithm can replicate; this is not a philosophy but a practice, not a theory but a way of moving through the world. It requires no certification, no institutional approval, no expert validation. It requires only the modest courage to be authentically yourself in a world that profits from your conformity.

The path forward, a new way of leading on the horizon, can be hyper-personalization: some can move ahead, others can feed an appetite for more questions, and still others can seek help. In the past, a thirty-person classroom would not have allowed the teacher to spend time addressing individual bottlenecks. Now, however, the student and employee who needs the "guide by the side" has one—and this AI guide is infinitely patient and unfazed by the bizarre and basic human stupidity. The benefits are infinite.

But here's where most people get stuck, and it's where our education systems and organizations most spectacularly fail. Most of what we call innovation, digital transformation, or educational reform is theater. It's designed to look like change while keeping you dependent on external validation, standardized metrics, and hierarchical approval.

Before you can truly embrace firefly thinking in our AI-enhanced age, you need to recognize the reinvention racket—the elaborate performance of progress that keeps you from discovering your authentic light.

That's exactly where we're headed next, but once you see through the false glow of institutional innovation theater, you can never unsee it. That's when your real light begins to shine.

The fireflies in Costa Rica taught me that authentic illumination can't be faked, can't be forced, can't be standardized. It emerges from within when conditions are right. Our job—as educators, leaders, learners, and humans—is to create those conditions.

For ourselves. For each other. For a world that desperately needs more authentic light.

Time to glow.

CHAPTER 5

THE REINVENTION RACKET: BUZZWORDS VS. TRUE CHANGE

"Innovation is saying no to a thousand things."
— Steve Jobs

Signal from the Future: *The university proudly unveils its $100 million "Quantum Learning Lab." Meanwhile, students take most classes through free AI tutors on their contact lenses. The lab's primary use: a very expensive coffee lounge where students meet to discuss social media's use of the "digital soul"—the one thing their AIs can't experience for them.*

FIFTY-MILLION-DOLLAR FAÇADE

Two years ago, I walked into what was supposed to be the future of education. The marketing materials had prepared me: "Innovation Center," "School of the Future," "21st-Century Learning Environment." The building itself was an architectural marvel—fifty million dollars of glass, steel, and promises. Flexible furniture that could be arranged in endless configurations. A maker space with 3D printers, laser cutters, and robotics equipment. Computer labs that the principal proudly compared to "looking like something from Google." Music rooms with professional recording studios.

The principal met me at the entrance, practically vibrating with pride. "Welcome to the future of learning," he said, gesturing at the walls covered with inspirational quotes about innovation and creativity—the kind of motivational graffiti that transforms any educational institution into a cross between a corporate retreat center and a therapy waiting room. Vibrating with pride, he announced, "We are transforming education here."

As we began the tour, he rattled off buzzwords, and I remember thinking, *He's done this same talk before.* I didn't want to be rude, and I didn't have to worry about time on this particular day, so I allowed him to continue. Finally, unable to resist, I poked the bear and asked how much of the local world these students usually encounter on a typical day. After a smooth sidestep, he returned to discussing "design thinking" and "the future," with every phrase carefully chosen to signal that this was not like other schools. Rebranding tradition as a revolution.

Then I walked into the first classroom, and the brutal reality hit. Thirty students sat in perfectly straight rows, their backs rigid, their eyes forward. The teacher stood at the front of the room, clicking through a PowerPoint that could have been created in 1995. Students took notes silently, occasionally raising their hands to ask permission to speak. The "flexible furniture" was arranged in the same configuration that my elementary school classroom had been forty years ago.

"Where's the student-centered learning?" I asked quietly.

"Oh, we do that on Fridays," the principal replied without irony. "Innovation hour."

We continued the tour. Room after room revealed the same story. The 3D printers sat unused, covered in dust, because no one had time to integrate them into the curriculum. The maker space was locked—"training issues," the principal explained. The computer labs ran typing tutorials and basic word processing. In one room, students were filling out worksheets—actual paper worksheets—about "twenty-first-century skills."

The expensive interactive whiteboards displayed static slides. The tablets stayed in charging carts because "classroom management is easier without them." One of the innovation labs was half-filled with storage boxes rather than students building projects. Millions of dollars had built a museum of educational theater, a monument to the gap between rhetoric and reality.

But here's what concerned me the most: The principal genuinely believed he was revolutionizing education. He wasn't lying or being deliberately evasive. He'd convinced himself that the building was the change, the tools were the transformation, and the labels were the learning. He'd spent millions of dollars on props for a play no one was actually performing.

They had built a monument to educational deception—a gleaming theater where innovation was performed but never practiced. This wasn't one misguided school. This was a systematic mess on an industrial scale.

THE ANATOMY OF FAKE CHANGE

That school visit triggered months of investigation. I started seeing the pattern everywhere—corporations, nonprofits, government agencies, even innovative startups. The same story, different stages: massive investments in transformation that transformed very little, revolutionary initiatives that reinforced the status quo, and disruption that carefully preserved every existing power structure.

The reinvention racket works because it satisfies everyone's needs without requiring actual change. Leaders get to feel visionary. Consultants get paid. Employees get to attend workshops instead of doing harder work. Boards see impressive presentations. But nothing fundamentally shifts.

Here's how the racket operates, especially now that we can slap "personalized" on everything.

THE CONSULTANT INDUSTRIAL COMPLEX

The incentive structure is perfectly designed to perpetuate fake change. Consultants get paid for complexity, not simplicity. The eighteen-month "AI transformation journey" generates far more billable hours than teaching people to use ChatGPT effectively. The million-dollar "innovation strategy" beats the thousand-dollar suggestion to "stop having so many meetings."

I've watched consultants charge seven figures to recommend exactly what employees had been suggesting for years, just wrapped in fancier PowerPoints. They conduct endless stakeholder interviews, create impressive frameworks, design beautiful slide decks, and deliver recommendations that either state the obvious or propose changes so complex they'll never be implemented.

The small, effective changes—the ones that might actually work—don't sell. They're not flashy enough for leadership to champion, not complex enough to justify the consulting fees, not dramatic enough to put on a resume. So, instead, we get transformation theater.

AI Washing

Slapping "AI-powered" labels on existing systems and calling it innovation. I've seen "AI-powered learning analytics" that produce the same basic Excel charts we've had since 2000. "AI-enhanced curriculum" that's just digitized textbooks with a search function. "Intelligent tutoring systems" that are glorified multiple-choice quizzes with slightly better graphics.

The Magic Button Myth

Believing AI will solve human problems without changing human behavior. No algorithm can fix a culture that punishes curiosity. You cannot code your way out of compliance-based thinking. The fanciest AI in the world won't help if your organization still rewards conformity over creativity.

Dependency by Design

Using AI to make people more dependent, not more capable. Real AI integration amplifies human intelligence. Fake AI integration replaces human thinking with algorithmic compliance. When your AI tools make people ask fewer questions rather than better ones, you're doing it wrong.

THE PROMOTION GAME

Leaders are often promoted for launching initiatives, rather than sustaining change. By the time anyone realizes that the transformation didn't work, the champion has moved on to bigger things. The "Ten-Million-Dollar AI Initiative" looks great on a resume, even if it accomplished nothing.

How many executives have you seen be celebrated for starting something but never held accountable for finishing it? We throw parties for ribbon-cuttings but not for five-year sustainability reports. We reward the announcement, not the achievement.

THE MEASUREMENT TRAP

It's easy to measure inputs: dollars spent, hours trained, tools purchased, consultants hired. It's much harder to measure outputs: Can people do things they couldn't before? Are problems being solved that weren't before? Is value being created that wasn't before?

So, we measure what's easy and pretend it proves progress. "We've trained ten thousand employees in AI literacy!" But can any of them use AI to actually improve their work? "We've invested $5 million in innovation!" But has anything actually changed?

MEASURING WHAT MATTERS

Here's how to shift from measuring inputs to authentic progress using firefly wisdom:

1. **The Flash Pattern Method:** Like fireflies that signal through patterns, not continuous light:
    - Document "flash moments"—specific instances when someone applies new learning
    - Track pattern frequency: Are flashes increasing and becoming more synchronized?
    - Example: Instead of *"completed AI training,"* write *"Sarah automated her weekly report using AI, saving three hours."*
2. **The Darkness Test:** Fireflies only reveal their light in darkness. Similarly:
    - Measure performance during challenges, not comfort
    - Create "lights out" scenarios—remove familiar tools and processes
    - Ask, "What happens when the manual disappears?"
    - True learning shows up when scaffolds come down

3. **Chain Reaction Metrics:** One firefly's flash triggers another's. Measure:
   - Teaching moments: When does someone share their learning unprompted?
   - Replication rate: How many others adopt a new practice without a mandate?
   - Evolution indicators: Is the skill being adapted, not just copied?
4. **The Six-Month Glow Check:** Replace annual reviews with firefly cycles:
   - What couldn't you do six months ago that you can do now?
   - What problem did you solve that would have stumped you before?
   - Who have you helped learn something you've mastered?
5. **The Biomimicry Balance:** Nature doesn't measure growth by height alone:
   - Root depth (foundational understanding)
   - Canopy spread (influence on others)
   - Ecosystem health (team/community impact)
   - Regenerative capacity (ability to recover and adapt)

Remember: Traditional measurement asks, "How much?" Firefly measurement asks, "What's different?" One counts inputs; the other celebrates transformation. One measures compliance; the other tracks capability.

Stop measuring the darkness. Start noticing who's beginning to glow.

THE SEDUCTION OF BUZZWORDS

The reinvention racket has its own language, carefully designed to sound transformative while preserving the status quo. With the firehose of initiatives, advertising, and communication bombarding us, it's crucial to develop a filter. Here are the warning signs:

- **Innovation Lab:** A room where nothing gets invented, but everyone feels innovative.
- **Digital Transformation:** Same thinking, new devices.
- **Student-Centered Learning:** The teacher still does all the talking, but now there's an iPad involved.
- **Agile Methodology:** Taking six months to approve a two-week project.
- **Design Thinking:** Redesigning processes nobody wanted while ignoring what actually needs to change.
- **AI-Powered:** Usually means "we added a chatbot."
- **Metaverse Strategy:** Building virtual offices while your real ones fall apart.
- **Hybrid Work Model:** Everyone's back in the office anyway, but now there's a policy about it.

Some of you will have a more natural ability to spot this than others. Futurist, author, and strategist Scott Smith and co-author Madeline Ashby, in their book *How to Future*, called this "sensing and scanning."[47] They emphasize the importance of identifying signals of the future as soon as possible. I would add that it's equally important to learn from previous mistakes, when one accepts the jargon with the best of intentions, only to see the initiatives fall flat across the system.

GREEN LIGHT SIGNALS (REAL CHANGE EMERGING INDICATORS)

Green light signals are signs that indicate team members have autonomy and are prioritizing action over theater.

1. **Bottom-Up Energy**
    - Employees creating solutions without being asked
    - Informal learning networks forming organically
    - People teaching each other skills that management doesn't even know exist
    - *Signal: The intern teaching Excel tricks to the CFO*
2. **Permission-Free Zones**
    - Spaces where experimentation happens without approval cycles
    - Budget allocations for "figure it out" projects
    - Failed experiments celebrated in company newsletters
    - *Signal: "We tried this; it failed; here's what we learned" emails*
3. **Language Evolution**
    - New vocabulary emerging from practice, not PowerPoints
    - Old terms retiring because they no longer fit reality
    - People saying, "I don't know" more often than "best practice"
    - *Signal: The death of "synergy" and the birth of specific, actionable terms*

4. **Time Horizon Shifts**
    - Six-month learning cycles replacing five-year plans
    - Quarterly skills audits instead of annual reviews
    - "What expired this month?" becoming a regular question
    - *Signal: Strategic plans written in pencil, not stone*
5. **Cross-Pollination Patterns**
    - Marketing learning from maintenance
    - Engineers teaching artists (and vice versa)
    - Generational reverse mentoring happening naturally
    - *Signal: The twenty-two-year-old teaching the CEO TikTok strategy*

RED FLAG SIGNALS (INNOVATION THEATER INDICATORS)

These tend to be new or existing initiatives with grand fanfare but are largely abandoned within months. Artifacts are often dusty equipment sitting unused from last quarter's "revolutionary transformation" rollout that never actually transformed anything.

1. **Announcement Addiction**
    - Big launches with no follow-through
    - Press releases before pilot programs
    - "Revolutionary" initiatives every quarter
    - *Signal: The demise of abandonment of innovation labs*

2. **Credential Inflation**
    - New certificates for old skills
    - Badges for basic users
    - Mandatory training with no application plan
    - *Signal: LinkedIn profiles with forty-seven micro-credentials*
3. **Silo Reinforcement**
    - Innovation departments separate from operations
    - "Future of work" teams with no actual workers
    - Digital transformation led by people who don't use the tools
    - *Signal: The chief innovation officer who's never failed at anything*
4. **Metric Manipulation**
    - Measuring activity, not outcomes
    - Celebrating inputs over impacts
    - Dashboard addiction with no behavior change
    - *Signal: "We trained ten thousand people!" (but nothing changed)*

WHAT TO DO WITH THESE SIGNALS:

1. **Create a Signal Journal**

- Weekly capture: What's emerging vs. what's just louder?
- Pattern recognition: Which signals cluster together?
- Reality check: What actually changed behavior?

2. **The 3-6-9 Test**
    - Three months: Is anyone still talking about it?
    - Six months: Has behavior actually changed?
    - Nine months: Would it survive if the champion left?
3. **Follow the Energy, Not the Announcements**
    - Where are people gathering without being told?
    - What tools are being adopted without training?
    - Which problems are actually being solved?

The Ultimate Signal Test: Is this creating new possibilities or just new vocabulary?

The future rarely announces itself with fanfare. It usually starts with someone, somewhere, quietly doing something differently because the old way stopped working. The skill isn't spotting the loudest signal—it's noticing the persistent whisper that gradually becomes a chorus.

The collapse of "revolutionary" initiatives teaches us more than their launch presentations ever could. The question isn't "What's new?" but "What's actually different this time?"

THE INNOVATION STRUGGLE

IBM's Watson for Oncology spent billions to be marketed as revolutionizing cancer treatment, and hospitals worldwide bought in. The reality? By 2017, it was described by doctors as "unsafe" and "incorrect," according to internal documents. A physician at Jupiter Hospital in Florida told IBM officers: "This product is a piece of s—. We bought it for marketing and with hopes that you would achieve the vision."[48] Not just ineffective, but potentially harmful. The problem wasn't the technology but the theater. IBM marketed Watson as AI replacing oncologists when it was actually pattern matching with limited data. Hospitals spent millions on innovation theater while actual modern breakthroughs in radiology were happening in unglamorous startups with no marketing budgets. The lesson: The louder the innovation announcement, the less likely actual innovation exists.

Los Angeles Unified School District's iPad initiative—$1.3 billion to give every student an iPad—was heralded as "transforming education."[49] What happened? Students hacked them in week one, the curriculum software didn't work, and teachers weren't trained. Meanwhile, Summit Public Schools quietly built a personalized learning approach using basic Chromebooks and smart pedagogy. No press releases, no vendor lock-in, just teachers and technologists working together to solve real problems. The contrast is instructive: LAUSD performed innovation for headlines; Summit built innovation for impact. One made national news for its failures; the other quietly spread to 380 schools.

FIREFLY FLASHPOINT

Your last transformation initiative—how much did it cost?
What actually changed? Nothing?
That's not transformation. That's theater.

THE PSYCHOLOGY OF THE *RACKET*

Why do intelligent people continue to fall for innovation theater? Because the performance racket exploits our deepest organizational fears and desires.

Complexity feels like sophistication. When faced with messy human problems, a two-hundred-slide deck feels more substantial than a one-page solution. We conflate complicated with comprehensive, as if the weight of the binder correlates with the weight of the thinking. Simple solutions—"talk to each other," "trust your people," "stop having so many meetings"—feel almost insulting in their directness.

The racket also exploits our fear of being left behind. Every organization dreads being the Blockbuster in a Netflix world. So, when consultants promise "digital transformation," we buy it not because we understand it, but because we're terrified of missing it. Fear sells far more innovation initiatives than vision ever could.

There's also the comfort of delegation. Hiring consultants or outsiders to solve your culture problem feels like action. It's something you can announce, and it provides air cover, something to point to when asked, "What are you doing about it?" That it rarely works matters less than that it looks like leadership.

But perhaps most seductively, the racket lets us feel progressive without risking anything real. We can discuss transformation while preserving every existing power structure. We can advocate for change while changing nothing about ourselves. It's organizational virtue signaling—all the appearance of progress with none of the discomfort of actual growth.

Until we understand these psychological hooks, we'll keep getting caught.

One effective strategy to handle this is my Three-Layer Test.

THE THREE-LAYER TEST

When you encounter a new initiative or transformation program, run it through these three filters:

Layer 1: The Translation Test

What they say → What's actually happening

Take any buzzword-heavy statement and translate it into plain English. If the translation reveals nothing concrete, you've found theater.
Example:

- **They say:** "We're leveraging AI-powered analytics to create data-driven, personalized learning experiences."
- **Translation:** "We bought software that could achieve our objectives, but right now, we are unsure how this will pan out."
- **Reality check:** Identify team members whose learning and ability to do the job actually improved.

Layer 2: The Kindergarten Test

Explain the initiative like you're speaking to a five-year-old. You can easily do this using an AI prompt: "*Explain this to me as if I'm five.*" Let the AI give you feedback, and be honest. If it struggles, the initiative is probably nonsense.

- **Real change:** "We're helping kids learn by letting them build things that matter to them."
- **Fake change:** "We're implementing a holistic stakeholder-centric paradigm shift in pedagogical methodology."

If you need more than two sentences to explain what you're doing, you're probably not doing anything.

Layer 3: The Monday Morning Test

What will people actually do differently on Monday morning?

- **Theater:** "We're transforming our culture" (but Monday looks exactly like last Monday). It's incredible how many leaders are actually resistant to change. Once you split the narrative from the action, they often occupy two different universes. Many of the leaders I met while researching this book call themselves agile thinkers, yet when a big call emerges, they either freeze or are unable to activate the change needed.

- **Real:** "Starting Monday, no meetings before 10:00 a.m. so people can do deep work" (actual behavioral change).

This is the zone of real change, throwing the "Hail Mary." In the talks I give about being a principal and director of schools and think tanks, I'm often confronted with the reality that the biggest change I've ever made was pushing back the start time of school and incorporating a healthy and balanced start to the day. Now, I know that economic and work pressures for parents often make this impossible, but when we implemented this, we saw a dramatic improvement in focus, attention to detail, work quality, and output.

Each buzzword provides cover for the fundamental fact that nothing real is changing. They're linguistic camouflage for institutional inertia.

THE CORPORATE GRAVEYARD

When the reinvention racket meets reality, companies die. They also die expensively, surrounded by innovation initiatives and transformation consultants.

Blockbuster didn't fail because they couldn't see digital streaming coming. They actually launched their own online DVD rental service to compete with Netflix and famously turned down the chance to buy Netflix for fifty million dollars in 2000. Despite having thousands of stores and millions of customers, Blockbuster failed because they couldn't let go of their existing business model. While Netflix focused on subscription-based rentals with no late fees, Blockbuster clung to the very penalty system that customers hated. As documented in Gina Keating's *Netflixed*, Blockbuster had every advantage—brand recognition, customer base, resources—except the willingness to disrupt themselves.[50]

General Electric bet billions on becoming a "top-ten software company" through GE Digital, their ambitious attempt to transform from an industrial giant into a tech powerhouse. Despite massive investments in their Predix platform and new digital headquarters, the cultural transformation never materialized. As the *Wall Street Journal* reported, GE ultimately sold most of GE Digital's assets for $1.2 billion in 2018—a fraction of what they'd invested.[51] The company discovered that proclamations and innovation labs couldn't overcome 125 years of industrial DNA.

IBM spent years promoting Watson for Education as the future of personalized learning, partnering with major publishers and school systems. Yet by 2020, IBM had quietly shut down Watson for Education.[52] Why? As industry analysts noted, they focused on the technology instead of understanding how teachers actually work and what students actually need. The AI was sophisticated, but it couldn't overcome the reality that education transformation requires more than algorithms.

BlackBerry dominated the smartphone market with nearly a 50% market share in 2009, but they fatally misread where technology was heading. When the iPhone launched in 2007, BlackBerry's co-CEO famously dismissed it, saying, "It's OK—we'll be fine."[53] They spent years perfecting physical keyboards while consumers were embracing touchscreens. By 2016, BlackBerry had less than 0.1% market share, killed by their refusal to abandon what had made them successful.

I've repeatedly seen this same pattern in education. Schools spend millions on iPads for every student, leading to no improvement in learning outcomes. The tablets sit in closets, unused, because no one ever asked whether the problem was a lack of devices or a lack of imagination. Teachers who've been trained to deliver information from the front of the room now deliver the same information from the same position, just with an expensive screen in their hands.

Now it's happening with AI. I predict that schools and companies will spend fortunes on AI tools that will sit unused or underutilized, not because the students won't use them, but because schools will struggle to weave them into the curriculum that has existed unchanged for decades. The work will be the same, middle managers will struggle to adapt, and AI will supercharge their competitors.

The problem so often is that many are trying to enhance the existing system rather than redesign it.

They're using AI to make traditional tests easier to grade rather than questioning whether traditional tests measure anything worthwhile.

Companies are using AI to automate broken workflows rather than fix them. They're deploying chatbots to handle customer complaints faster rather than asking why they have so many complaints in the first place.

THE SIMPLE TRUTH THEY DON'T WANT YOU TO KNOW

Here's what the reinvention racket doesn't want you to realize: Real change is often simpler than fake change. It just requires more courage.

When Satya Nadella became CEO of Microsoft, the company had a toxic culture—competitive, political, and everyone was trying to prove they were the smartest person in the room. He didn't launch a "cultural transformation initiative." He didn't hire consultants to create a two-hundred-slide deck on organizational change.

He changed one thing: the hiring and promotion criteria. Instead of rewarding know-it-alls, they started rewarding learn-it-alls. That's it. No consulting fees. No change management programs. No year-long rollouts. Just: "We hire people who want to learn, not people who think they know everything already."

This shift exemplified what Carol Dweck calls the growth mindset: "In a growth mindset, challenges are exciting rather than threatening. So rather than thinking, 'Oh, I'm going to reveal my weaknesses,' you say, 'wow, here's a chance to grow.'"[54]

That single change cascaded through the organization. People who thrived on politics left. People who thrived on learning stayed. The culture transformed not through initiatives but through selection. Microsoft went from irrelevant to essential, from closed to open, from knowing to learning.

Real change is often a single decision courageously implemented. Fake change is a thousand initiatives that avoid the one decision that matters.

THE FIREFLY TEST FOR AI

So, how do we know if our AI initiatives are real transformation or expensive theater? Apply the firefly test:

- **Does it create more light or just rearrange the shadows?** Real AI integration enables people to generate their own insights more effectively. Fake AI integration makes them more dependent on algorithmic outputs. If people are asking better questions, taking more risks, thinking more creatively, that's real. If they're following more protocols—waiting for AI approval, thinking less for themselves—that's theater.

- **Is the light self-generated or externally powered?** Real transformation teaches people to use AI as a bicycle for the mind, amplifying their intelligence. Fake transformation treats AI as a replacement for thinking. Are your people learning to prompt, guide, and collaborate with AI, or are they learning to submit to it?

- **Does it spread or require constant maintenance?** Real change creates chain reactions. One person learns something powerful and can't wait to share it. Energy builds. Fake change requires constant external motivation, endless training sessions, and persistent compliance monitoring. Which pattern do you see in your organization?

THE UNCOMFORTABLE AUDIT

Here's an exercise that might be painful but will help. Think about your organization's biggest innovation investment over the last two years, the thing you spent the most money on, got the most excited about, and told everyone would change everything.

Now answer honestly:

- Can anyone demonstrate a skill they couldn't perform before?
- Can anyone point to work they're doing differently—not talking about doing differently, not planning to do differently, but actually doing differently today?
- Has any meaningful metric actually improved?
- If the initiative disappeared tomorrow, would daily operations change at all?

If the answer to these questions is no, you've been funding theater. And the longer you pretend otherwise, the further behind you'll fall while competitors who embrace real change pull ahead.

BREAKING FREE FROM THE RACKET

The good news? Once you see the reinvention racket, you can't unsee it. Real transformation becomes possible once you stop playing along, but it requires the courage to let go. A clear pattern has emerged from every successful school transformation I've been a part of, whether working with educators on the Great Barrier Reef or helping redesign curriculum in major cities such as Sydney or Beijing. The work never begins with a new initiative; it begins with an honest audit. Together, we had to first distinguish performance from progress and compliance from capability. It wasn't about destroying the old—some traditional elements served real purposes. It was about finding the courage to stop pretending the performance mattered.

Real transformation means:

- Admitting when something isn't working, even if you spent millions on it.
- Choosing simple solutions over impressive ones.

- Measuring outcomes, not activities.
- Rewarding results, not initiatives.
- Having the courage to stop performing and start progressing.

When we transformed our traveling school's curriculum, real change didn't come from adding new technology or hiring consultants. It came from letting go—of standardized tests, of time-based metrics, of the illusion that learning could be measured in hours seated.

Some of our most powerful learning experiences occurred completely tech-free in the Okavango Delta of Botswana, where students collected scientific data, sat with local elders, learned oral histories, and practiced the ancient art of storytelling around the fire. No Wi-Fi, no PowerPoints, no innovation frameworks—just humans learning from humans, nature teaching through experience.

One evening, as I watched students present their research through stories rather than slides, decode the constellations and stars, and solve problems through conversation rather than Google, I realized that we'd been adding layers of complexity to something beautifully simple. Learning happens when curious humans engage with the world. Everything else is just expensive decoration.

We didn't throw out everything. Some traditional elements served real purposes…

WHEN REAL CHANGE HAPPENS

When I spoke at TEDx in Shanghai (in collaboration with Duke Kunshan University), I made the argument that we need to insert trust back into our system and build community around things like passion, purpose, and mastery—but most importantly, on trust.[55] From what I've seen, when we trust young people and our staff members with real responsibility, when we give them hope in that learning journey, they rarely let us down.

To watch Russell Cailey's Ted Talk, scan the QR code:

Finland's education transformation didn't happen overnight. The reforms began in the 1970s and took decades to implement fully. Initially, there was significant debate—not panic—about moving away from tracked education systems and standardized approaches.

Finnish educators and policymakers engaged in extensive planning and gradual implementation. They developed a clear framework: highly trained teachers (all with master's degrees), national curriculum guidelines with local flexibility, and trust in professional judgment over standardized testing.

The international community wasn't worried—they were skeptical. Many dismissed Finland's approach as too idealistic for larger, more diverse nations. Even within Finland, the changes required sustained political consensus across multiple governments.

What emerged over the next decades astounded the world. Finnish students ranked consistently high in international rankings while spending less time in school. They developed deep learning without standardized tests. They achieved excellence through trust, not control.

That's a real transformation: a simple principle, courageously sustained, spreading naturally because it works. Not adding layers of oversight but removing barriers to good teaching. Not complicating the system but clarifying the purpose: let learning happen.

The irony? Countries around the world now spend millions trying to copy Finland's "model," creating frameworks, consultants, and initiatives to reproduce something that succeeded precisely because it rejected frameworks, consultants, and initiatives.

Real change is often that simple. And that's hard.

THE TRUE COST

The reinvention racket isn't just expensive—it's exhausting. Every fake transformation makes people more cynical about real change. Every failed initiative makes the next one harder to believe in. Every million spent on theater is a million not spent on actual improvement.

Worse, it wastes our most precious resource: human enthusiasm. People start their careers eager to make a difference. After years of participating in transformation theater, they learn to keep their heads down and play along. The very people who could drive real change learn instead to perform fake change.

But here's the firefly truth: Authentic light is always more powerful than artificial illumination. A single person genuinely transforming their work inspires more change than a thousand PowerPoints about transformation. A small team actually using AI to solve real problems creates more value than a massive "AI Center of Excellence" that produces only reports.

THE END OF INNOVATION 1.0

The real casualties of the reinvention racket aren't budgets or buildings—they're the humans ground down by endless rounds of fake transformation.

I've watched it happen too many times. Brilliant educators who once stayed late experimenting with new approaches now stay late filling out "assessment rubrics," with the spark in their eyes replaced by a kind of professional numbness. They've lived through Digital Transformation 1.0, the 21st Century Learning Initiative, and the STEM Revolution and are now facing the AI conundrum.

Each promised revolution delivered more paperwork, more compliance theater, more elaborate ways to do exactly the same thing.

These aren't lazy people or resisters of change without cause.

These are the ones who cared, who tried, who believed.

But after the third transformation that transformed nothing, something broke. They learned to protect themselves by expecting nothing. Hope becomes dangerous when it's repeatedly crushed by initiative after initiative that changes everything except what matters.

In every school, every company, every organization I've visited, there's this same minefield followed by a graveyard of good ideas killed by innovation theater. Simple suggestions buried under complex frameworks. Practical solutions suffocated by process. The enthusiasm of those who saw what needed changing was slowly extinguished by committees, consultants, and endless postponement.

What haunts me most? Leaders complain about cynical employees, never recognizing that they created them. Every failed transformation doesn't just waste money—it teaches people that real change is impossible. Innovation fatigue isn't just tiredness. It's learned helplessness. It's the organizational equivalent of that moment in Tokyo when my students chose test prep over discovery, now stretched across entire careers.

The real cost can't be measured in dollars. It's in the creative energy that goes into appearing busy rather than being useful. It's in the bright minds that learn to hide their light because it's safer than watching another committee extinguish it. It's in the gradual dimming of human potential, one failed initiative at a time.

If Innovation 1.0 was about adding—more tools, more processes, more complexity—then Innovation 2.0 is about subtracting. Strip away the theatrical elements. Remove the barriers between idea and implementation. Delete the committees that exist to create other committees. Innovation 2.0 does not ask, "What can we add?" but "What can we remove to let natural creativity flow?" It's not about million-dollar transformations but thousand-dollar experiments. It's not about changing everything, but changing the one thing that matters. The future belongs to organizations brave enough to do less, but to do it real.

YOUR CHOICE

You face a choice. You can continue funding the reinvention racket—hiring consultants, launching initiatives, buying tools that won't be used, and measuring inputs instead of outcomes. You can continue to perform transformations while avoiding actual change.

Or you can step off the stage.

There's nothing wrong with hiring quality consultants to ease a particular pain point, but my advice is to always open an avenue for internal learning and development.

Start small. Pick one real problem. Use simple tools. Measure actual outcomes. Let people experiment without elaborate frameworks. Reward results, not rhetoric. Have the courage to admit when something isn't working and stop doing it.

Here's what that fifty-million-dollar school taught me: The building didn't matter. The technology didn't matter. The buzzwords didn't matter. What mattered was whether anyone was learning, thinking, and growing differently. And they weren't.

True light takes work. Cheap flashes don't last. The reinvention racket promises easy transformation through expensive initiatives. Real change requires harder choices but simpler solutions.

The firefly doesn't need a fifty-million-dollar habitat to glow. It just needs the courage to generate its own light, the wisdom to rest between flashes, and the authenticity to illuminate what matters.

You have power over your glow, not external validation. Realize this, and you will find your light.

Perhaps it's time to stop performing change and start creating it.

YOUR REINVENTION AUDIT

Before you move to the next chapter, conduct your own honest assessment:

What's something in your life or organization that looks impressive from the outside but doesn't actually create real change?

What would you replace it with if you prioritized impact over appearance?

Sometimes, the most revolutionary act isn't adding something new—it's having the courage to stop pretending the old thing works.

The racket ends when we stop buying tickets to the show.

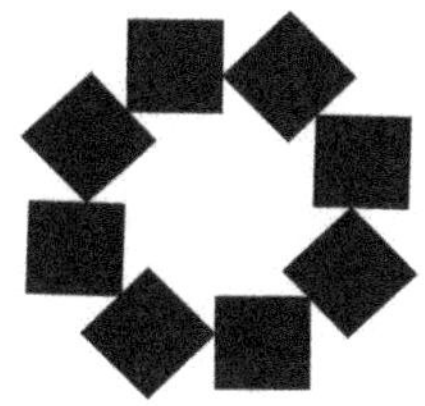

CHAPTER 6

HOLDING ON & LETTING GO: BRIDGING WISDOM & INNOVATION

"The best way to predict the future is to create it."

— Peter Drucker

Signal from the Future: *Grandpa still hand-carves wooden toys while his grandson 3D prints identical ones in seconds. At the craft fair, people line up for Grandpa's creations, paying 100x more. "The algorithm can't code soul into things," a buyer explains, running her fingers over the imperfect edges.*

THE GREAT DIVIDE

I'm noticing a pattern of finding myself in increasingly uncomfortable meetings at the companies I advise. At many meetings, I am faced with people who might have thirty or forty years of experience in whatever job they're doing, who have certain ways of doing their job, certain ways of managing, transferring information, and working systems that might have been in place for decades.

The veterans of these organizations are becoming increasingly confused and tense about discussing the company's DNA, special relationships, sacred knowledge, and how information should be passed down through the organization.

There's wisdom in many of these systems. A patience and flow, along with a whole web of how internal structures operate and exist for and within the community. This is incredibly valuable and must be treasured despite the confusing times we now collectively occupy.

However, on the other side of the table from these veterans, I often find tech consultants, tech evangelists, or IT departments that have now been empowered with the onset of new tools, new frontiers, and, obviously, artificial intelligence.

Often, the people promoting solutions don't sync with the community or how that place works. So, when people from the technological world come in and start discussing specific algorithms, adaptive assessments, and scaling AI to reach millions of customers potentially instantly, it creates a gap.

I recently attended an AI conference in the United Arab Emirates, where a tech founder spoke on the influence of AI on education. He clearly meant well, but you could sense the divide emerging between him and the audience in the room. His self-plaudits of how many companies he had sold and how many patents he had designed were meant to establish his credibility, but the crowd wanted tools. They wanted forecasts. They wanted answers. The result was that a gulf emerged between this well-meaning tech creator and the people he was trying to serve.

Often, when you enter the arena like this, you feel like you almost have to pick a side—or at least, the people in the meeting expect you to pick a side. They'll look at you as if to say, "Hey, come over to our side of the argument." Usually, it's either that the tech is moving too fast or the world of learning and education is moving too slow. But here's what I've learned: The moment you pick a side, you've already lost. The real opportunity isn't in the "tech versus tradition" debate—it's in finding the synchronization point where human wisdom and technological capability amplify each other. The answer isn't slowing down tech or speeding up education. It's creating a new rhythm entirely.

FATHER OF THE FOREST

Te Matua Ngahere—the Father of the Forest. I'd spent a decade bouncing between the world's great cities, finding my rhythm in their concrete designs. Nature was something I'd appreciated intellectually: Botswana's star-rich skies, Iguazu's thundering waters. Beautiful, yes. But home? Not really. That was Tokyo's neon pulse, Mumbai's chaos, Dubai's vertical ambitions.

Then came a morning when our Māori guides welcomed us to Waipoua Forest in New Zealand. "You don't visit Te Matua Ngahere," they explained. "You are received by him."

The ceremony began before we could see anything through the pre-dawn mist. Ancient chants moved through the darkness, speaking directly to something primal within us. As we walked, our guide shared how this kauri tree had stood here for two thousand years—through the rise and fall of empires, through the birth of religions, through humanity's journey from bronze to blockchain.

When we finally stood before him—and yes, *him*; this was undeniably a presence, not just a tree—I felt something crack open in my city-hardened soul. Here was a teacher who didn't need Wi-Fi. Here was wisdom that emerged through stillness, not strategy.

Our guide gestured toward the massive trunk. "He teaches us about time," she said. "Not human time—always rushing, always measuring. Tree time. The patience to grow deep before growing tall."

As I thought about our students pushing to excel in Silicon Valley or embrace the intensity of Wall Street, I reflected on what it is about us in our daily lives that wants to keep racing, to keep up with not just appearances but every new platform and every trending influencer's perspective, I also reflected on my own addiction to productivity metrics and growth hacks.

Yet here stood proof that some wisdom can't be downloaded. Some presences can't be virtualized. You have to bring your body to it—feel the mist on your skin, let the ancient chants rewire your nervous system.

Te Matua Ngahere had weathered approximately two thousand years of storms. He'd survived by bending, not breaking, by growing in community—root systems intertwined in an underground network of mutual support. Did we really think technology invented networks? These trees had been sharing resources and warnings through mycorrhizal connections for millennia.

That morning taught me what indigenous knowledge offers our hyperconnected age: True innovation honors ancient wisdom. We don't need to choose between roots and rockets. The glowworms that would illuminate the forest that night weren't competing with LED screens. They were offering something screens never could: the magic of ephemeral, embodied presence.

THE FALSE CHOICE

Here's the challenge: How do you preserve the deep wisdom of an organization or community while adopting technology that could amplify its impact? Too often, we frame this as an either/or choice—but it doesn't have to be.

Often, given time and the right supportive environment, both sides can come together. I've found that when resistant teachers see what technology can do for students—demonstrated respectfully, without dismissing their concerns—they recognize its power to enhance storytelling and learning. Beyond the technology itself, we must show how human flourishing remains central. Even dissenting voices will acknowledge that humanity is what matters most.

Yes, machines can capture our notes, replicate our thought patterns, and conduct our research. But living it? That remains uniquely human.

WHAT WE MUST KEEP

So, let's dive into what I think deserves to be kept and what needs to be let go. Let's begin by looking at what we could keep.

Wisdom and Discernment

First is knowing which information serves life itself. Artificial intelligence, for example, can generate infinite content, but only human wisdom can discern what matters. Indigenous cultures worldwide understand something we've largely forgotten in our big cities: Data without wisdom is just noise.

In Kolkata, I learned from the New Light organization, whose innovative approach empowered local women through education, dignity, creative expression, and peer support in ways that transformed my understanding of how people truly grow. Their methodology went beyond data collection or case management systems. It was grounded in wisdom, understanding that rebuilding self-worth must come before any skill-building or formal education can take root.

The core values weren't written in textbooks but lived through patient, daily acts of restoration. No algorithm could determine when a girl was ready to trust again, when she could look someone in the eye, when she had healed enough to imagine a different future. That discernment—knowing which intervention serves life at which moment—comes only from human wisdom.

In Botswana, Maun-based author Bonty Botumile educated our nomadic learners on how crucial information has been transmitted across generations through oral storytelling. Sitting around campfires in the Okavango Delta, I watched how our guides helped us weave complex knowledge into narratives—not just facts about animal behavior or seasonal patterns, but wisdom about how to live, how to resolve conflicts, and how to maintain harmony with the environment.

These stories carried survival information, cultural values, and practical knowledge, all wrapped in memorable narratives that no written manual could match. The information was inseparable from its human context, from the relationship between the storyteller and the listener, from the trust built up through generations of this practice.

I reflect today on the nights spent by the Thamalakane River. On how today AI can now store an infinite number of facts about the Okavango Delta and Tswana society, but only human wisdom knows which stories need to be told when and where, which lessons a particular group of young people needs to hear, and which ancient narrative speaks to today's challenges.

Emotional Intelligence

Second is reading the room, feeling the moment. Sure, technology and AI can analyze the text, but they can't feel the energy shift. It can't discern when a young person or a colleague has had a breakthrough. It can't sense when someone needs encouragement rather than a challenge. This is uniquely human.

When we launched the educational programs in Botswana, thirty students joined us, bringing their own learning traditions and perspectives. We trialed ten days without technology, which became an unexpected gift. Instead of seeing it as a limitation, we discovered how the absence of screens created space for deeper connections and indigenous knowledge-sharing.

What we initially saw as challenges became our greatest teachers. The young people showed the adults how project-based learning could be enriched by incorporating local wisdom traditions, oral storytelling circles, and community-based problem-solving methods we'd never encountered before. During this period, we created something deeper: core values like "Ikigai" (putting your soul into your work), "satya" (living by truth), and "kaizen" (continuous improvement). We saw all these concepts activated beyond action plans and design circles, allowing a powerful collective illumination to take place.

What made community building work wasn't the structure or the content—it was reading each student's readiness, sensing when they were overwhelmed versus when they were ready to be pushed further. When you give young people hope in the learning journey, they rarely let you down—they almost always rise to the occasion.

This human ability to sense emotional readiness is backed by research. According to Dr. Marc Brackett from Yale's Center for Emotional Intelligence, educators with high emotional intelligence tend to have students with better grades, increased engagement, and lower stress levels.[56] Research showed that emotionally intelligent educators create classrooms with improved academic achievement and better classroom behavior. But what AI-enhanced data can't capture is that moment-to-moment sensing, knowing that this particular student, on this particular day, needs this particular type of support. That's the irreplaceable human element.

Sacred Relationships

Third is the bond between teacher and learner, between athlete and coach, between employee and mentor. For thousands of years, humans have transferred complex wisdom through relationships. We now have the tools that can deliver information in milliseconds, but they can't create trust. It can't create vulnerability, and it's connections that make deep learning and progress possible.

The importance of sacred relationships became clear to me during college admissions. I'd struggled terribly in high school, and my exhausted mother accompanied me through the application process. My transcript was mediocre at best—one reviewer generously called it "mildly impressive." Then I met a sociology teacher who saw past the data. In our brief encounter, she connected the subject to my life, to my mother's story, to questions I didn't know I was carrying. She saw potential where others saw averages. Seven years later, I returned to teach sociology at that same school.

She could have simply handed me a course catalog. All the information was there. But what ignited change was human connection—her patience with a lost student, her gift for making abstract concepts personal. This is what our students truly seek: not just information, but relationships that honor their trust. No algorithm can replicate that transformative moment when a teacher sees potential instead of problems, when trust opens the door to real change.

CULTURAL INTUITION

Understanding context cannot be programmed. Trust me, I've lived in Japan. I've lived in India. I've lived in many places where context is king, and a single mistake on a cultural level can be fatal for business relationships. Every great leader I know has the ability to read between the lines. They understand what's said, and more importantly, what is not being said. They can navigate the unspoken rules that help human communities thrive.

HSBC's famous "Eel" advertisement (easily located on YouTube) brilliantly captured this truth.[57] It featured an English businessman at dinner with Chinese clients in a Chinese restaurant. When served eel, he eats every bite, thinking that he needs to finish his food to be respectful. However, to his Chinese counterparts, this is a signal that they have not provided him with enough food, so, much to his dismay, they then bring out a second plate of eel. The campaign's core message was that cultural differences in business require more than translation—they require deep local knowledge and understanding.

This isn't just about avoiding embarrassment. In cross-cultural business settings, I've learned that communication goes far beyond words. Silence might indicate deep consideration in one context and disagreement in another. Gestures and expressions carry meanings that vary not just between cultures but within them, depending on relationships, hierarchy, and context. No AI can parse these subtleties—they're not in any database. They emerge from lived experience, relationships, and the dynamic nature of human interaction.

This isn't just about avoiding embarrassment. As the world becomes smaller, business hubs of influence are emerging in different places than they did a generation ago. Lagos drives West African finance, São Paulo shapes Latin American innovation, Mumbai powers global services, and Dubai connects East and West. Success in these markets requires more than translation—it demands understanding when formality matters and when it doesn't, how relationships build trust differently across contexts, and why the same proposal might need completely different framing in Seoul versus Stockholm. But even more important than learning protocols is understanding when to use them—and when silence speaks louder than any words could.

THE POWER OF STORY

I feel we've all become embarrassed by narrative, often dismissing it as inefficient when compared to data. We now have the tools to process data very quickly and efficiently. However, it's humans who can weave the stories. These are the stories that stick in the heart, that change behavior. In my experience, every great leader is first and foremost a storyteller.

HP's Garage:

In 1939, Bill Hewlett and Dave Packard started their company in a one-car garage in Palo Alto with $538. Their first product? An audio oscillator bought by Walt Disney Studios for *Fantasia*. That garage is now considered the birthplace of Silicon Valley. The story isn't about the technology—it's about two friends who believed in starting where you are with what you have.

3M's Failed Sandpaper:

In 1902, five businessmen founded Minnesota Mining and Manufacturing (3M) to mine corundum for sandpaper. The mine was worthless—the mineral was actually low-grade anorthosite. A complete failure. But instead of giving up, they pivoted, learned, and experimented. Today, 3M holds over a hundred thousand patents. Their origin story teaches that failure isn't final if you keep innovating.

Airbnb's Cereal Boxes:

When Brian Chesky and Joe Gebbia couldn't pay rent in 2007, they rented air mattresses in their apartment during a design conference. To fund their struggling startup in 2008, they sold forty-dollar boxes of Obama O's and Cap'n McCain's cereal. They made thirty thousand dollars selling breakfast cereal.[58] Today, Airbnb is worth billions. The story reminds us that resourcefulness matters more than resources.

Stories have the power to ignite the spark, empower change, and set the wheels in motion. Personally, I'm obsessed with a good origin story.

Ask yourself, do you know the origin story of the business you work for? Do you have a diary of the origin story of the business you founded? Do you know the origin story of the school or university you attend? If not, look it up.

The fusion of ancient wisdom and modern tools isn't abstract philosophy—it's happening now with measurable impact. Take Te Hiku Media's Papa Reo project in New Zealand, which has created AI speech recognition for Te Reo Māori. The platform was trained on decades of recordings from native speakers, but crucially, the Māori community maintains complete sovereignty over their language data, not big tech companies. The AI handles the processing scale needed for modern voice-activated technology, while elders and language experts ensure cultural protocols are preserved. Young Māori can now speak to their devices in their ancestral language, helping reverse language decline. As Te Hiku Media states, this approach ensures the benefits derived from these technologies go directly to their communities.[59] [60]

In education, the Green School in Bali manifests this fusion physically. The campus is built primarily from bamboo using traditional construction techniques, creating an architectural statement about sustainability. Students pursue international curricula while surrounded by structures that demonstrate environmental principles through their very design. The school deliberately integrates modern technology education with local cultural values and environmental practices. This isn't about choosing between tradition and innovation—it's about proving they can strengthen each other.

WHAT WE MUST RELEASE

Now let's look at what we should release. What should we let go of? What can the technology handle?

Here's the rewrite with only verifiable facts:

Information Gathering

When information was scarce, we needed human specialists to find, organize, and catalog knowledge. Now AI can research faster and more comprehensively than any human. The shift is clear: Let AI handle data gathering so humans can focus on making meaning and synthesizing.

The Associated Press demonstrated this in 2014 when they began using automated writing software for corporate earnings reports.

Previously, journalists spent hours producing these routine reports. After automation, AP could produce thousands of earnings stories each quarter instead of hundreds.[61]

The key outcome: AP didn't replace journalists with machines. Instead, they freed reporters from repetitive data processing to focus on investigative work, analysis, and finding the real stories behind the numbers. The automation handled routine reports while humans focused on what required judgment and context.

That's the pattern: Technology handles volume, humans handle meaning.

Pattern Recognition for Routine Decisions

AI is better than humans at spotting trends in large data sets, optimizing logistics, and handling predictable scenarios. So, let's free up some human brainpower for the unpredictable, the creative, and the unprecedented.

Radiology shows us what this shift looks like. As of 2023, the FDA has cleared over 750 AI algorithms for radiology, representing 76% of all medical AI approvals.[62] These systems excel at pattern recognition: flagging potential pneumothorax on chest X-rays, detecting pulmonary nodules, and identifying areas of concern in mammograms. The AI doesn't replace radiologists—it triages the routine cases, allowing doctors to focus on complex diagnoses where human judgment matters most. When an algorithm spots something unusual, that's when twenty years of medical training kicks in. The technology handles pattern matching in thousands of normal scans. The human handles the puzzles that could save lives.[63]

Credit card fraud detection has undergone a similar evolution. Modern systems process millions of transactions per second, utilizing machine learning to identify patterns, including unusual locations, atypical purchase sequences, and spending anomalies. The algorithms automatically flag obvious fraud patterns. However, complex cases—such as legitimate emergency purchases, unusual travel patterns, and business accounts with erratic but valid activity—still require human analysts. The system catches the patterns. Humans provide the context. One handles volume; the other handles nuance.

The principle remains constant: Let machines excel at pattern recognition in large datasets. Reserve human intelligence for the unprecedented, the ambiguous, and the creative.

Drafts and Templates

AI can generate first attempts and messy prototypes. It can put together a slide deck of presentations. For you teachers out there, it can create the lesson plan, but that isn't what you submit. That isn't what you run with. That is your dirty, messy prototype.

Think of it like a sous chef doing the prep work. They've chopped the vegetables, measured the spices, and laid out the ingredients, but you're still the chef who decides how much heat to use, when to add each element, and how to adjust for today's diners. The AI gives you the raw materials more quickly than you could gather them yourself. You provide the artistry.

I've watched brilliant educators spend entire weekends crafting lesson plans from scratch, agonizing over structure, searching for the right examples. Now they can generate a solid framework in minutes and then spend those reclaimed hours on what actually matters—thinking about how Priya in the third row learns differently than Marcus in the back, finding that perfect local example that will make abstract concepts click, preparing for the unexpected questions that make teaching magical.

It's your job to add salt to the process, context, and your own wisdom, which can transform generic content into a meaningful connection. Generic becomes specific. The template becomes tailored. The skeleton becomes a living lesson. The point is to allow the technology to assist us with initial drafts and templates, because every hour we don't spend on formatting is an hour we can spend on transformation.

The Human Core

Scheduling, data entry, compliance reporting—AI handles these tasks better than humans. This should be embraced, not resented.

I know the resistance. I've felt it myself. Handing over tasks we've always done feels like surrender. But here's what I learned: Every hour I spent color-coding spreadsheets was an hour I wasn't spending with students. Every report I manually compiled was a conversation I didn't have.

Ask any teacher about their biggest frustration, and you'll hear the same refrain: "I became a teacher to teach, not to fill out forms." Doctors face the same crisis—spending more time with electronic records than with patients.

This isn't noble suffering—it's a systemic waste of human potential.

Let technology manage some of the bureaucracy. Let it schedule the meetings, track the attendance, and generate the compliance reports that no one reads anyway. Not because these tasks don't matter, but because humans matter more. They can once again manage and push forward with relationships, critical thinking, and creativity.

Here's the critical distinction: We're releasing tasks, not responsibility. We're automating processes, not purpose. The human remains at the center, using technology and artificial intelligence as a thinking partner, not as a replacement.

You're still accountable for the outcomes. You're still the one who decides what matters. But now you have time to actually do what matters. That's not loss—that's liberation.

FIREFLY FLASHPOINT

When did efficiency become our only god?

CORPORATE FUSION: WHEN ANCIENT WISDOM MEETS MODERN TOOLS

Let's look at integration and cross-disciplinary learning. What could it look like when organizations hold on to wisdom yet embrace modern tools and technology?

Patagonia: Environmental Stewardship Through Technology

Patagonia built its entire business model around the indigenous principle that we don't inherit the earth from our ancestors but borrow it from our children. The company implements its "Supply Chain Environmental Responsibility Program" at facilities worldwide, using tools like the Higg Index to measure and reduce the environmental impacts of manufacturing. It incorporates technology to analyze supply chain decisions and improve the durability and sustainability of products through materials research. Every technological insight gets filtered through their core principle: What would future generations want us to do? Technology amplifies wisdom—it doesn't replace it.

Salesforce: Digital Ohana

Marc Benioff built Salesforce's entire culture around the Hawaiian concept of "ohana," meaning extended family, where everyone belongs and no one gets left behind. Trust is the foundation of their relationships with employees, customers, partners, and communities. They integrate technology throughout their platform to enhance customer service, analyze cases, and provide personalized responses. However, the technology is designed to strengthen human relationships, not replace them. The tools serve the ohana principle—using data to better understand customer needs so they can serve their extended "family" more deeply.

This fusion of ancient wisdom and modern tools is already happening, creating powerful new models for learning. It can be seen in the physical world, where technology enhances timeless craftsmanship.

At the University of Stuttgart's "SmartLab," for instance, artisans use augmented reality to guide their woodworking, receiving step-by-step digital instructions directly in their field of view. Imagine this same technology in the hands of a master carpenter in Japan, teaching the ancient art of *"kigumi"* joinery. The AI could project a complex design onto a piece of wood, guiding an apprentice's hand with digital precision. The technology creates the perfect guide, but the final fit, the feel of the wood, and the soul of the craft remain purely human.

This principle of fusion extends beyond physical crafts to social philosophies. The Zulu concept of Ubuntu—"I am because we are"—offers a powerful blueprint for designing collaborative AI. Instead of creating isolated, individual learning paths, technology guided by this philosophy would serve the group's collective growth. The AI could handle the logistics and resource management, but its primary function would be to strengthen the human bonds that make learning stick.

We see a similar pattern in long-standing educational models that are now being amplified by technology. Montessori schools, for example, have emphasized personalized, passion-driven learning for decades. Now, technology can enhance this core mission. An AI can observe a child's learning patterns and suggest real-time resources, but it does so in service of the Montessori philosophy that children learn best when they follow their natural curiosity. The technology provides new tools, but the child still chooses their own adventure.

THE FIREFLY INTEGRATION PROCESS

How do we hold on to what matters while letting go of what's expired, especially when the world is moving so quickly? What follows is the firefly integration process for this current age.

Step One: The Light Source

What wisdom actually guides you? Not what I think should guide you, not what looks good on a LinkedIn profile, but what deep principle actually shapes your decisions when technology conflicts with your values?

Growing up in the United Kingdom, I never quite fit into my own skin. School was torture until 3:00 p.m., when the bell freed me to pursue my real education: meticulously painting Napoleonic soldiers, losing myself in my father's crime novels, uncovering my grandfather's wartime stories from Malaya. The chasm between what fascinated me and what school offered revealed a serious failure. Our education systems had become monuments to disconnection—static, stagnant, and utterly divorced from what young people actually care about.

My journey across six continents taught me something profound: Every person and place carries wisdom, and authentic learning happens through relationships, not curricula. As I worked with students and teachers worldwide—training educators, building innovation labs, prototyping new approaches, designing strategies for schools—one principle emerged clearly: Wisdom flows in all directions.

When you allow people to have some skin in the game, when you build community around concepts they feel passionate about, that's when transformation happens. I saw metrics rocket when such initiatives were implemented—engagement, autonomy, and belongingness significantly increased. This happened not through technology, but through honoring a simple wisdom: learning happens when people care about what they're learning.

Step Two: Identify the Deadwood

What structures in your organization, in your life, no longer serve the light? What policies, practices, or habits worked in the pre-AI world but now block that very thing you're trying to create?

A special note for those of you in older institutions: The older an institution grows, the more it tends to gather rules, laws, and policies, so you guys might be more at risk or may have a heavier lift at identifying the deadwood than a new startup or a company in its infancy.

I am very proud of how, during my journey, I let go of being the expert in the room. I now have no barriers at all to letting students lead, and I no longer feel the need to dictate everything that goes on in a learning space. Growing up in a very traditional academic setting, I learned that good teachers and mentors don't necessarily have all the answers.

Now, with the current technology, the best teachers are the best learners. I've had to release my ego and pride as my own first principle, which is that I do not need to be an expert all the time.

Step Three: Finding Fusion

Where can ancient wisdom guide modern technological capabilities? Where can AI tools amplify ancient wisdom? Honor indigenous knowledge?

AI can be used to research and organize ideas, but wisdom is still best taught through story—that's how humans actually learn. Technology can connect learners, but human rituals create the sense of belonging that is a prerequisite to learning. For years, I put this into practice by borrowing a technique directly from the Dallas Cowboys NFL team. At the start of every significant session, we held a morning huddle—a brief, consistent ritual designed to build community and release tension before the real work began.

Each morning, while music plays, everyone has to greet each other in a huddle and let go of any tension or friction from the previous day's work and collaborations. Whether with a fist bump, a hug, or a high five, the rule is that everyone has to greet each other over the course of a three- to four-minute song.

No one gets left behind.

And in that moment, any tension is released.

That's the agreement. And at the start of an academic term or a year, we all look each other in the eye and ask, "Can we do this? Can whatever happened in the dorm, on the project, whatever fight or friction there was, be released in this morning ritual?" And every young person looks me in the eye and says, "Yes," and that's what they do.

Step Four: Test the Glow

Does the fusion point create a more authentic light? Are people more capable, more connected, more alive, or are we just making the old look new? Are we attaching new labels? Real integration creates a coherent glow. When ancient wisdom and innovation come together, they amplify each other rather than compete.

Here's how to test if you're creating real light or just rearranging shadows:

The Monday Morning Test: If your integration were to disappear tomorrow, would anyone notice? When we introduced AI tools at one school, teachers initially used them to generate lesson plans more quickly. But nothing changed in the classroom—same teaching, same outcomes. That's fake fusion. Real fusion happened when teachers used the time saved to have one-on-one conversations with struggling students. The technology served the relationship.

One time, I forgot the ritual and didn't play the music. My learners quickly snapped, "Play the song. Let's do this right." That's the Monday morning test.

Energy Audit: Walk into any space where fusion is happening. Do people seem more alive or more exhausted? When technology truly serves wisdom, it creates energy. People lean in, their eyes brighten, and conversations spark. When it's just theater, you see the opposite—glazed eyes, forced enthusiasm, and people counting minutes until they can escape. When I moved our start time to 10:00 a.m., the Energy Audit was real. My learners came alive, and I saw the impact of a simple shift in the routine.

Multiplication: Real integration spreads without mandate. One teacher discovers a way to use AI that honors their teaching philosophy, and suddenly, others are asking, "How did you do that?" No training required, no compliance monitoring. The light attracts more light. If you need constant reinforcement and rules, you've created dependency, not integration.

THE HUMAN REALITY

I'll be honest. When this new technology of artificial intelligence entered my professional setting, the narrative was that we would all become obsolete. That narrative persists to this day, but working with educators across the world has taught me something profound.

Technology can actually make poor practice painfully obvious and great teaching irreplaceable. When we use tools correctly to prepare our reports, meeting minutes, other research, and content organization, it's very clear that relationships are the human moments—and part of any planning should be to maintain that human magic.

Technology has made me a better educator, a better human, a better professional, and now a better businessperson. It handles what I don't really want to do. It handles the mundane so I can focus on what I want to do: the creative.

So the question isn't whether technology and artificial intelligence will replace the human connection; it's whether human educators will use technology to become more deeply human.

THE CURRENT CHALLENGE

The ubiquity of artificial intelligence has the potential to create problems. How will universities react when they're being charged high fees and professors are using artificial intelligence to generate lectures? How will workplaces react when employees' latest pitch decks or reports are AI-generated? What tricks will we employ to make it seem as if AI wasn't used?

We're often in danger of creating a false choice, and this potentially destroys our ability to learn and lead effectively. We believe we must choose between wisdom and innovation, between tradition and technology, between honoring the past and building an AI-enhanced future.

I see real danger ahead. When organizations rush to create AI monitoring policies, approved product lists, and compliance frameworks, they often destroy the very thing they're trying to protect. I've watched colleagues turn into AI detectives, scrutinizing each other's work for signs of "cheating." This has led to accusations flying, trust eroding, and relationships crumbling. The tragedy is that in our panic to control the technology, we abandon ethics and forget to ask *why* we're using it in the first place. We become so obsessed with policing the tools that we forget their purpose: to amplify human capability, not diminish human connection.

But what if the choice itself is the problem? What if the most powerful learning actually happens when ancient wisdom meets AI innovation or when timeless principles guide cutting-edge tools? That's potentially where the magic can happen.

THE INTEGRATION CHALLENGE

I want to end this chapter and this arc with a challenge that, I hope, will make you a little uncomfortable—because, if you're not uncomfortable, you're not ready for the integration.

Can you name one ancient wisdom tradition that guides your work? Something deeper than business best practice, or an AI optimization list or technique?

____

____

____

____

Can you name a principle that connects you to thousands of years of human learning?

____

____

____

____

Next, name one way you're currently using it or planning to use it. One application, one process, one system. How are you implementing this wisdom?

____

____

____

____

Finally, name one way technology betrays that wisdom. What technology are you using that goes against the principle you have identified? Your integrity depends on resolving this tension—not next year, not when the AI or the technology gets better, and not when someone gives you permission, but now.

____

____

____

____

Here's what I know: Leaders and learners who thrive today won't be those who use the most AI, the most technology. It won't be those who avoid it completely, either. It'll be those who weave ancient wisdom and sacred knowledge with AI and technological capabilities so skillfully that we can't tell where human insight ends and machine intelligence begins.

BUILDING THE BRIDGE

Here's what I've learned from watching organizations trying to integrate the latest technology. Most actually fail because they keep the wrong things, and then they release the wrong things. They hold on to outdated structures—maybe due to personal preference, maybe due to ego—while potentially abandoning timeless principles.

In many corporate settings, we are in danger of pitting one side against another: Those who want to travel very quickly, very fast, a million miles an hour, with the technology, and those who would prefer to go a little slower.

We need people who can dance between both worlds and help others do the same. The firefly insight here is that AI can amplify the magic, but it can't create it. What we must do as a community—and, I hope, as a community reading this book together—is learn how to make the light impossible to ignore.

ARC THREE
SUSTAINED GLOW:
TOOLS FOR AGENCY & ACTION

"It does not matter how slowly you go as long as you do not stop."
— Confucius

We've done the hard work together. We've diagnosed why the old systems are failing—the collapse of time, the performance theater, and the death of wonder and curiosity. We've started building the new framework around firefly thinking that's self-powered, regenerative, and contagious. We've exposed the fake innovators wasting billions while showing how to bridge ancient wisdom with cutting-edge tools.

But here's where most books end and most people get stuck.

They walk away inspired, maybe even equipped, but they don't actually change anything. They go back to waiting for permission, to planning instead of building, to letting the daily pressures extinguish their curiosity.

That's not going to be you.

These next three chapters aren't about understanding or believing. They're about doing. We're entering the sustained-glow phase, where theory becomes practice, frameworks become action, and firefly thinking becomes a way of life that changes everything around you.

> **Chapter 7: Stop Waiting, Start Owning** is about taking ownership—not waiting for someone else to fix the problems you see, but claiming them as yours to solve. I'll give you the tools that successful builders carry and challenge you to make your first chess move before you finish the chapter.
>
> **Chapter 8: Beyond Reimagination** moves beyond reimagination to systematic building. We'll turn your ownership into real solutions that solve actual problems for actual people, providing you with strategic frameworks for choosing your battles, building your alliances, and leveraging technology to accelerate everything you're passionate about. No more planning meetings. It's time to build.
>
> **Chapter 9: Keeping the Explorer Alive** tackles the long game. How do we keep our explorer's spirit alive when the building gets hard, success tempts you toward complacency, or pressure to optimize threatens to kill your wonder?

Here's what's at stake.

We're preparing for a future where spaces become catalysts for societal change. Where AI handles routine thinking so humans can focus on the creative and meaningful. Where old hierarchies dissolve into dynamic learning communities. A future where society values giving 70% instead of grinding out 100%. Imagine what we could create with that extra 30%.

We're creating a world where digital avatars might win prizes humans currently chase and occupy spaces humans currently fill. Where human biology merges with technology. Where quantum learning environments make today's classrooms look as antiquated as a horse and cart.

The question isn't whether these changes will happen. They're already happening.

The question is whether you'll be an explorer who shapes the future or a bystander who gets shaped by it.

Your firefly light isn't just personal illumination. It's collective navigation in uncertain, choppy waters. We need people who never stop glowing, never stop building, never stop exploring.

So, let's stop talking about change and start creating it. Let's move from sustained inspiration to sustained action.

It's time to build. It's time to embrace the future.

And it's time to start now.

CHAPTER 7

STOP WAITING, START OWNING: TAKING AGENCY IN THE AGE OF CHANGE

"One day you'll leave this world behind,
so live a life you will remember."

— Avicii

Signal from the Future*: The city council schedules another hearing for 2037 about approving residential fusion reactors. Kim doesn't wait—she crowdfunds a neighborhood microgrid that's operational in six weeks. The council is still debating permit requirements when Kim's block becomes the first energy-independent street in America.*

THE PERMISSION ADDICTION

I need to tell you something that's going to make you uncomfortable.

You're a permission addict, and it's killing your potential. While you wait for approval to innovate, someone else is already building your obsolescence. The permission slip you're waiting for? It expired the day AI learned to code.

Martin Seligman's groundbreaking work demonstrated how repeated exposure to uncontrollable situations trains people to stop trying, even when they actually have control.[64] There is also extensive research on the "locus of control," Julian Rotter's concept that describes whether people believe they control their own fate (internal locus) or that external forces determine their outcomes (external locus).[65] Studies consistently show that those with an external locus of control wait for permission, while those with an internal locus create their own opportunities.

It would be an interesting first step for firefly thinkers to see how many employees wait for annual or quarterly reviews to make changes versus those who act independently. Recent workplace studies suggest that 73% of employees feel they need explicit approval before implementing new ideas, even small ones.[66]

This paradox plays out constantly in business history. IBM famously passed on personal computers initially. Xerox invented the computer mouse and graphical interface, but didn't commercialize them. Kodak invented digital photography and then shelved it.[67]

Why? Because innovation through proper channels requires permission from people whose success depends on the status quo. But innovation through ownership requires only courage and evidence.

I personally have seen this nervousness manifest during my work: "I'd love to, but…" followed by a list of external barriers. There's also the never-ending issue of time spent seeking consensus versus time spent building. The data on this is staggering. According to Microsoft's recent Work Trend Index, the average employee now spends nearly 70% of their time on communication—email, chats, and meetings—leaving little room for creative and focused work.[68] The report also found that employees ranked ineffective meetings as their number one productivity disruptor, highlighting a massive disconnect between activity and actual progress.

We need to be on the lookout for a paradox unfolding in the modern workplace: the rise of micromanagement and decreasing autonomy, even as tools become more sophisticated. Gartner, one of the world's leading research firms, reports that 38% of employees feel they have less autonomy now than they did before the pandemic. This feeling is mirrored at a global scale. The 2023 Global Innovation Index paints a similarly complex picture: While corporate R&D spending remained high, the report highlights a sharp decline in venture capital funding and warns that the future of innovation is "fraught with uncertainty."[69] In other words, simply investing in more technology is not automatically translating into more innovation or empowered workers.

Right now, somewhere in your mind, you're thinking, *This firefly stuff sounds great, but... I need my boss to buy it first, for example, to try the "Firefly Wheel,"* or *I'll start this after I get more training,* or *Once the organization is ready for change, then I'll begin.*

You're waiting for someone to hand you a permission slip to transform learning. To innovate a classroom. To redesign your team approach. To change your leadership style. To build something that matters.

But here's what I learned while watching communities across six continents: The changemakers who actually move mountains never wait for permission.

They say, "I'm going to own this problem, and I'm going to solve it."

Not "I'm going to study this problem." Not "I'm going to reimagine this problem." Not "I'm going to ideate forever around this problem." Not "I'm going to advocate for solving this problem." Not "I'm going to wait for the conditions that are absolutely perfect to then start solving this problem."

They say, "I'm going to own this and solve it, starting now."

That's the mindset the firefly effect is pushing. As a bonus, I'm not just going to look for problems and solutions. I will be an active participant and leader in forming the idea, designing the blueprint, and building the systems. And in doing this, I'll support and enable the growth required.

That's what separates the dreamers from the builders. That's what separates the fireflies from the flickering bulbs.

Ownership.

THE OWNERSHIP SHIFT

What I want to show you now is the difference between permission seeking and ownership taking. This reframe changes everything.

So, what might we find if we explore permission-seeking behavior? Here are a few examples of such thinking:

- Can I try a different approach?
- What happens if the system doesn't support this?
- I need more resources before I can start.
- Someone should really do something about this.

Let's reframe this to ownership-taking behavior. What might we find here? Here are just a few examples of ownership-taking statements:

- I'm going to test this approach and measure the results.
- I'll work within the current constraints while building evidence for change.
- I'll start with what I have, and I'll prove the concept.

- I'm going to solve this problem.

Here's the crucial insight: In our rapidly changing world, where artificial intelligence can generate solutions in milliseconds and global communities can form overnight, the bottleneck is not resources or permission.

Do you know what the connection is between the Filet-O-Fish at McDonald's, Starbucks' café latte, and the Sony PlayStation? They all had origin stories driven by people who took ownership and embarked on their own little side quests. No permission slips. No grand corporate strategies. Just individuals who saw a problem and decided to solve it.

The Filet-O-Fish: When "No" Means "Not Yet."

In 1962, Lou Groen owned a McDonald's franchise in Cincinnati with a problem: sales plummeted every Friday because his Catholic customers couldn't eat meat. Corporate said no to his fish sandwich idea—they were testing their own meatless option, the "Hula Burger" (grilled pineapple with cheese, seriously).

But Groen didn't wait for permission. He kept experimenting in his own kitchen, perfecting a fish sandwich. When Ray Kroc finally agreed to a sales competition—Hula Burger versus Filet-O-Fish—Groen's creation sold 350 sandwiches. The Hula Burger? Six.[70]

The ownership moment: Groen could have accepted corporate's "no" and watched his business struggle each Friday. Instead, he owned the problem and solved it. Today, the Filet-O-Fish generates over three hundred million dollars annually.

The Café Latte: Vacation Inspiration Meets Ownership.

In the early 1980s, Howard Schultz was just Starbucks' marketing director when he traveled to Italy. He was captivated by Italian coffee bars—the community, the craft, the experience. He returned, bursting with ideas to transform Starbucks from a coffee bean retailer into something revolutionary.

The owners said no. They were in the business of selling beans, not experiences.

Did Schultz wait for permission? No. He left to start his own coffeehouse, Il Giornale. Two years later, he acquired Starbucks and transformed it into what we know it as today.[71] The café latte—that Italian inspiration—became the foundation of a one-hundred-billion-dollar company.

PlayStation: The Project Nobody Wanted.

In the early 1990s, Ken Kutaragi, a Sony engineer, saw his daughter playing Nintendo and thought that Sony could do better. One problem: Sony's leadership had zero interest in video games. They were a serious electronics company. Games were toys.

Kutaragi didn't wait for approval. He developed the sound chip for Nintendo's Super Nintendo in his spare time, which got Sony's attention. Even then, most executives opposed entering the gaming industry, but Kutaragi kept building, kept proving, and kept pushing.[72]

The PlayStation launched in 1994. Gaming is now one of Sony's most profitable divisions, generating over twenty-five billion dollars annually.

THE PATTERN OF OWNERSHIP

Notice the pattern? None of these innovations came from strategic planning sessions. None had official approval. All faced active resistance. But they happened because someone decided to own a problem.

The people who acted weren't rebels or rule-breakers. They were ownership takers. They saw something broken and decided that fixing it was their responsibility, regardless of whether they had permission or not.

It's ownership.

The tools have evolved. The tools have changed. And the tools, if used correctly, have empowered us greatly. Therefore, the future belongs to people who see problems and think, "That's mine to solve," not "Someone should handle this."

FIREFLY FLASHPOINT

That permission slip you're waiting for?
You're holding it. You've always been holding it.

THE THREE OWNERSHIP LEVELS

Let's explore the three ownership levels that separate those who wait from those who build:

Level One: Personal Ownership.

Take responsibility for your growth and learning. No more waiting for training programs and the perfect conditions. You become the architect of your development, using every resource available—from AI tutors to online communities to real-world experimentation.

Remember from Chapter 1 how skills now expire every eighteen months instead of every thirty years? That's why personal ownership matters more than ever. You can't wait for your company's annual training budget or your school's curriculum update. By then, the skills you need will have changed again. As we explored in Chapter 3, when students chose test prep over discovery at that Tokyo startup showcase, they were surrendering their personal ownership to a system that measures compliance, not capability.

The shift occurs when you claim your learning journey, as seen in the students in Botswana we discussed in Chapter 4, who embraced Ikigai—putting their soul into their work. They didn't have perfect conditions. They had ownership.

Level Two: Project Ownership.

See a problem in your sphere of influence and claim it. Don't just identify it. Don't just complain about it. Own the solution. This is where you move from personal growth to creating value for others. You spot a broken process, an unmet need, a gap in the system, and you say, "I'm going to fix this."

This is exactly what we saw in Chapter 5 with the Associated Press automation story. Individual journalists didn't wait for industry-wide transformation. They spotted a problem—spending 20% of their time on routine earnings reports—and owned the solution. They automated data gathering so humans could focus on meaning-making. No permission from the journalism establishment. Just ownership of a specific problem.

Or think back to Chapter 2's discussion of performance versus progress. How many meetings have you sat through where everyone expresses concern about a problem, but no one claims ownership? Project ownership means moving from the great pretend to the great build.

Level Three: Systems Ownership.

Take responsibility for transforming the environment where you operate. This is where firefly thinking creates cultural change. You're not just solving one problem—you're changing the conditions that create problems. You're building new systems, new cultures, new possibilities.

This is what we explored in Chapter 6 with Patagonia and Salesforce. They didn't just solve individual problems. Patagonia didn't just make better jackets—they built an entire business model around the indigenous principle that we borrow the Earth from our children. Every decision, every innovation, every use of technology serves that systems-level ownership.

Remember Satya Nadella's transformation of Microsoft from Chapter 5? He didn't launch another innovation initiative. He changed one thing at the systems level: hiring and promoting learn-it-alls instead of know-it-alls. That single change cascaded through the entire organization.

This is also what the Finnish education system did, as we discussed in Chapter 5. They didn't just improve teacher training or update textbooks. They took systems ownership by completely reimagining what education could be when you trust professionals instead of controlling them.

The Three Levels of Ownership

From Personal Agency to Collective Impact

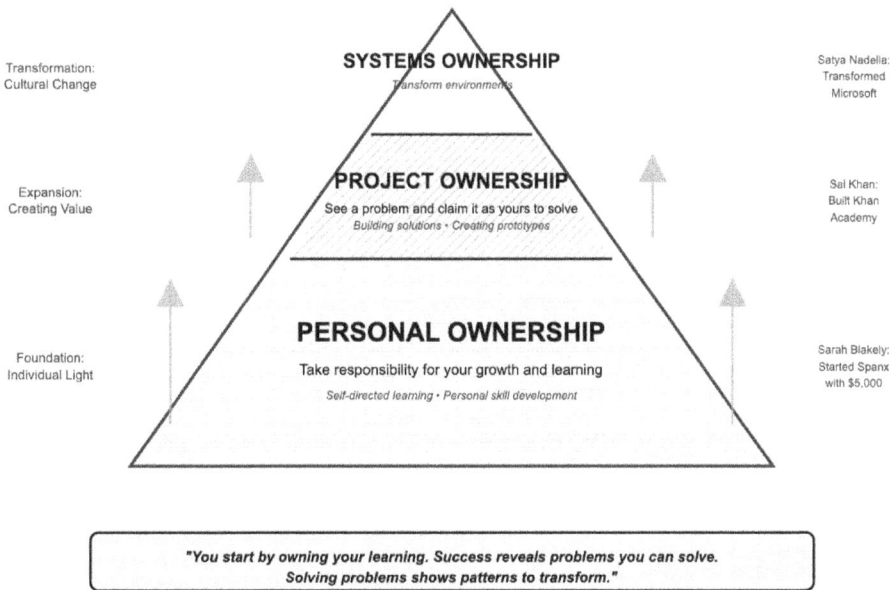

Transformation:
Cultural Change

SYSTEMS OWNERSHIP
Transform environments

Satya Nadella:
Transformed
Microsoft

Expansion:
Creating Value

PROJECT OWNERSHIP
See a problem and claim it as yours to solve
Building solutions • Creating prototypes

Sal Khan:
Built Khan
Academy

Foundation:
Individual Light

PERSONAL OWNERSHIP
Take responsibility for your growth and learning
Self-directed learning • Personal skill development

Sarah Blakely:
Started Spanx
with $5,000

"You start by owning your learning. Success reveals problems you can solve. Solving problems shows patterns to transform."

Figure 4: The Three Levels of Ownership - From Personal Agency to Collective Impact. This pyramid illustrates the natural progression of ownership-taking. Level 1 (Personal Ownership) forms the foundation—taking responsibility for your own growth and learning. Level 2 (Project Ownership) emerges when you claim specific problems as yours to solve. Level 3 (Systems Ownership) represents the transformation of entire environments. Real-world examples show this progression: Sarah Blakely started by solving her own wardrobe problem, Sal Khan began tutoring his cousin before building Khan Academy, and Satya Nadella transformed Microsoft's entire culture. Each level builds on the previous, creating expanding circles of impact.

FROM ROOTS TO CANOPY: THE OWNERSHIP SPIRAL

The progression is natural. You start by owning your learning (Level One). Success there reveals problems you can solve (Level Two). Solving enough problems shows you the patterns in the system itself (Level Three). Each level builds on the last, creating a spiral of expanding ownership and impact.

As we saw with Te Matua Ngahere in Chapter 6, that two-thousand-year-old kauri tree, growth happens by going deep before going tall. Personal ownership is your root system. Project ownership is your trunk. Systems ownership is your canopy, creating shelter and possibility for others.

Now, let's be real. Most people never move past Level One. They take ownership of their personal development but ultimately wait for someone else to fix the systems around them. They become highly skilled individuals trapped in broken environments, like Formula One drivers stuck in traffic.

But the people changing the world? They operate at all three levels simultaneously. They're constantly learning (Level One), always building solutions (Level Two), and consistently transforming systems (Level Three).

Remember: The obstacle to effective learning advances us on our journey.

What dims your light becomes the reason you glow brighter.

THE BUILDER'S BACKPACK

Let me give you the exact tools you need to move from reimagination to redesign, and then finally to building. I call this the "Builder's Backpack"—five essential tools for taking ownership in any given situation.

Tool One: Bravery Anchored in Principle. Not reckless risk-taking, but courage rooted in your core values. Remember Chapter 6, where ancient wisdom became a compass? When you know what you stand for, you can act even when the path isn't clear. This is because your core principles act as an anchor.

Think about it: Every great builder in history had principles that guided them when they took risks. They weren't gambling—they were acting from a place of deep conviction. When your actions align with your values, what looks like risk to others feels like integrity to you.

Firefly insight: Just as fireflies use bioluminescence—an internal chemical reaction—your principles are your internal light source. You can't borrow someone else's principles any more than a firefly can borrow another's glow. Remember how, in Chapter 4, we talked about self-powered light? This is where it begins.

Builder's prompt: What principle would I defend even if it cost me? What belief lights me up from within? Write it down. That's your North Star when the path gets dark.

Tool Two: Prototype Thinking. Move away from perfect planning to messy building. This is also an extremely playful mindset. Now, AI can help us generate dozens of approaches in minutes. Don't spend months perfecting one idea. Build, test, and iterate rapidly. The feedback from real users beats theoretical planning every time.

I've watched too many brilliant ideas die in planning committees. Meanwhile, someone with a prototype—messy, imperfect, but real—changes everything. In the time it takes to create the perfect plan, a builder has already tested ten versions and found what works.

***Firefly insight**: Fireflies don't plan their light show—they flash and adjust based on response. Each flash is a prototype, testing what attracts mates, what warns predators, and what signals safety. As we discussed in Chapter 5 about the reinvention racket, real change is often simpler than fake change. A prototype beats a PowerPoint every time.*

Builder's prompt: *What could I build in the next 48 hours that would teach me more than six months of planning? Stop reading after this chapter and build it.*

Tool Three: Scientific Obsession. Become mildly, slightly obsessive about understanding what actually works. Try to measure everything, or at least most things. Document the patterns you see when you're prototyping. Use digital tools to track your results. The most successful builders I've ever worked with are those who combine bold vision with obsessive attention to data.

I once heard someone say that data is now the new gold. It's hard to argue with that, but here's the key: It's not about drowning in metrics; it's about finding the few measurements that actually matter and watching them like a hawk.

Firefly insight: *Scientists studying fireflies discovered that different species have distinct flash patterns. Some do double flashes, while others do long glows, each perfectly timed. They're not random; they're precisely coded communications. Your data obsession should be similar, not measuring everything but decoding the patterns that matter. Remember our discussion in Chapter 1 about the collapse of time? In a world where everything expires in eighteen months, pattern recognition becomes survival.*

Builder's prompt: *What's the one metric that, if it improved, would make everything else easier or unnecessary? That's your firefly frequency. Track it obsessively.*

Tool Four: Emotional Resilience. Here's what few people tell you about building: It's emotionally brutal. Rejection, criticism, failure, and setbacks are normal. Stress, bitterness, and anger do no one any good, including yourself.

Build an emotional toolkit. Use meditation apps. Lean into support networks. Try to give things perspective because, in time, those criticisms, rejections, failures, and setbacks won't feel as brutal. In line with the theme of the book, protect your firefly light from burnout.

The builders who last aren't the ones who don't feel the pain. They're the ones who've learned to process it, learn from it, and keep moving despite it.

Firefly insight: *Fireflies don't glow continuously—they flash and rest, flash and rest. This isn't weakness; it's sustainability. As we explored in Chapter 3 about the death of wonder, burnout happens when we forget that creativity requires regeneration. Your emotional resilience isn't about being tough—it's about honoring your cycles.*

Builder's prompt: *What rituals help me regenerate after setbacks? What restores my glow? Build these into your routine* ***before*** *you need them. As we learned from the morning greeting ritual in Chapter 6, sometimes the smallest practices can create the biggest resilience.*

Tool Five: Strategic Humor. Try not to take yourself too seriously. The most effective change agents I know and have worked with often use humor not only to disarm resistance but also to build connections. They also use it to maintain perspective. Laughter isn't frivolous. It's strategic and also infectious.

When you can laugh at the absurdity of the systems you're trying to change, you rob them of their power to intimidate you. When you can find humor in your mistakes, you become more human and relatable. People follow builders who can laugh, not martyrs who only suffer.

Firefly insight: *In some species, fireflies synchronize their flashing until entire trees pulse with light. Humor works the same way—one genuine laugh can sync an entire room. Remember from Chapter 2 about performance versus progress? Humor cuts through performance.*

It's hard to pretend when you're genuinely laughing. It reveals the authentic human beneath the role.

Builder's prompt: *What's absolutely ridiculous about the problem I'm trying to solve? Find the absurdity. Share it. Watch how it transforms resistance into curiosity. Like those fireflies in Southeast Asia that turn whole trees into light shows, your humor can turn whole organizations into possibilities.*

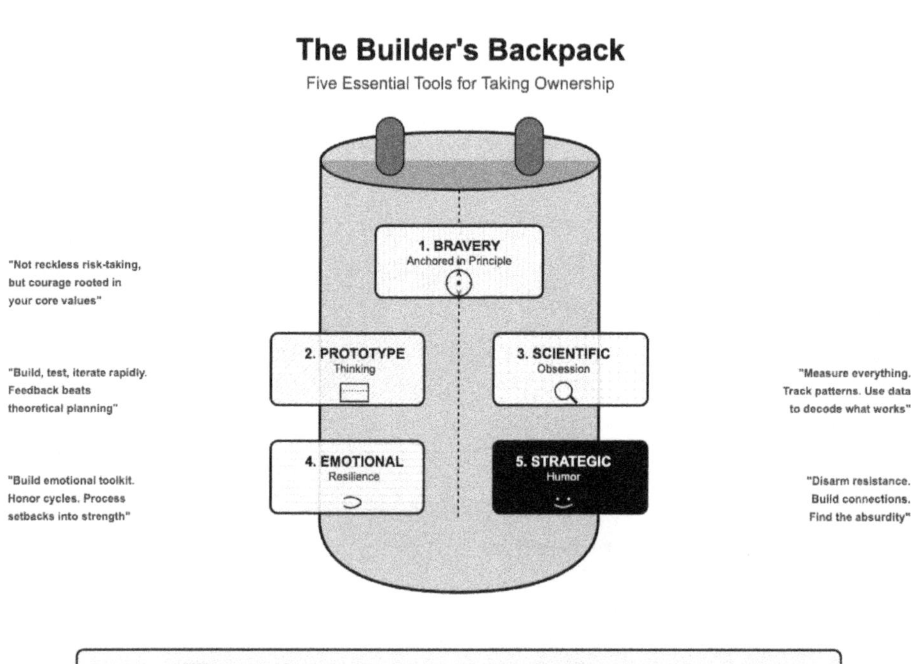
The Builder's Backpack
Five Essential Tools for Taking Ownership
1. BRAVERY
Anchored in Principle
"Not reckless risk-taking, but courage rooted in your core values"
2. PROTOTYPE
Thinking
"Build, test, iterate rapidly. Feedback beats theoretical planning"
3. SCIENTIFIC
Obsession
"Measure everything. Track patterns. Use data to decode what works"
4. EMOTIONAL
Resilience
"Build emotional toolkit. Honor cycles. Process setbacks into strength"
5. STRATEGIC
Humor
"Disarm resistance. Build connections. Find the absurdity"
"These aren't separate tools—they work together. Your principles give courage to prototype. Your prototypes generate data. Your data helps you know when to rest. Your rest gives perspective for humor."

Figure 5: The Builder's Backpack - Five Essential Tools for Taking Ownership. Like any journey into unknown territory, building in the age of AI requires the right equipment. This backpack contains five interconnected tools: (1) Bravery Anchored in Principle—your moral compass for navigating uncertainty, (2) Prototype Thinking—the ability to build rough versions quickly, (3) Scientific Obsession—rigorous tracking of what actually works, (4) Emotional Resilience—the springs that help you bounce back from setbacks, and (5) Strategic Humor—the ability to find lightness in the journey. These tools work synergistically: your principles give you courage to prototype, your prototypes generate data to analyze, your analysis reveals when to rest, and rest provides perspective for humor.

THE BACKPACK INTEGRATION

These aren't separate tools—they work together like firefly swarms. Your principles give you the courage to prototype. Your prototypes generate data to obsess over. Your data helps you know when to rest and regenerate. Your regeneration gives you the perspective to find humor. Your humor attracts others to join your principled work.

As we learned from Te Matua Ngahere in Chapter 6, the strongest trees grow in a community, with root systems intertwined. Your Builder's Backpack isn't just for you—it's for creating the conditions where others can build, too.

Final builder's prompt: *Which tool in my backpack is strongest? Which needs development? As we discussed in Chapter 4 about the firefly mindset, you need all five types of light. A firefly that can only flash once isn't going to change the darkness.*

Now, these aren't just *nice* ideas.

They are tools that separate successful builders from perpetual reimaginers, those who are addicted to reimagination, ideation, and endless planning.

Put these into your backpack; you'll need all five on your journey.

HORIZON SCANNING FOR TOMORROW'S BUILDERS

Here's what's on the horizon right now while people are waiting for permission. As futurist Amy Webb notes in her book *The Signals Are Talking*, the future doesn't arrive fully formed—it emerges from weak signals that compound into transformation.[73] The question isn't whether these changes will reshape how we learn, lead, and thrive in the age of AI. The question is whether you'll be scanning the horizon as a builder or watching from the sidelines.

Let's apply horizon-scanning principles to domains important to most of us in our daily lives. As William Gibson famously said, "The future is already here—it's just not evenly distributed."[74]

In Education: Learning in the Age of AI.

Thousands of teachers are already creating AI-enhanced learning experiences in their classrooms without waiting for district approval. They're using free tools, sharing resources in online communities, and proving what works through student results.

Now, the critics might say, "Well, that's just because of a lack of policy, and as soon as regulations are in place, that will stop." But here's what horizon scanners know: Regulation follows innovation, not the other way around. I've seen teachers build entire project-based curricula using AI planning tools—planning field trips, creating project arcs, designing assessments, and structuring community showcases—not to make life easy, but to enhance both their professional experience and student outcomes.

No permission. No budget increase. No committee approval. Just teachers owning these tools and enhancing creativity. Student engagement scores are increasing. Connection to the material is deepening. Consider the data from Alpha School, where AI-personalized learning has improved outcomes by two times while reducing student anxiety.[75]

This is what "learning in the age of AI" actually looks like—not waiting for perfect systems but building better learning experiences with available tools.

In Corporate Innovation: Leading When Everything's Changing.

Teams are using no-code platforms and AI systems to build solutions without IT approval. Changes that used to take years now happen in weeks. They're not asking permission. They're building prototypes, demonstrating value, and getting retroactive approval.

I spoke with a marketing team at a Fortune 500 company that is using AI to personalize customer communication in ways their customer relationship management system cannot handle. Instead of waiting for software upgrades, they built a workaround that increased response rates by 300%. Then IT asked them to teach other departments.

This is horizon scanning in action. Citing Scott Smith again, he writes in his book *How to Future*, effective leaders don't predict the future—they sense and responde to emerging possibilities.[76] These teams sensed that AI could solve their problem today, not in three years when the official upgrade arrived.

In Community Building: Thriving Through Connection.

Parents are creating micro-schools using online platforms and shared resources. They're not waiting for educational reform. They're building alternatives that help their communities thrive.

Peter Schwartz, the legendary scenario planner, calls this "having the art of the long view"—not waiting for the future but actively creating it.[77] These parent builders understand something crucial: in the age of AI, thriving isn't about having the most resources. It's about creating the most connections.

THE HORIZON SCANNER'S ADVANTAGE

Here's what these builders understand that permission-seekers don't: we're living through what futurists call a "phase transition"—when the old rules dissolve and new possibilities emerge.[78] In phase transitions, the advantage goes to those who act on weak signals rather than waiting for strong confirmations.

The tools for transformation have democratized:

- AI that once required millions now runs on smartphones.
- No-code platforms let anyone build applications.

- Global communities form around shared challenges instantly.
- Knowledge that took years to acquire can be accessed in minutes.

As Jane McGonigal writes in her book *Imaginable*, the future belongs to those who can think the unthinkable and do the undoable.[79] But here's the key: you can't think the unthinkable while waiting for permission. You can't do the undoable by following approved procedures.

YOUR HORIZON SCANNING TOOLKIT

To truly learn, lead, and thrive in the age of AI, you need to develop horizon-scanning capabilities:

1. **Signal Spotting:** What emerging tools could solve your current problems? Don't wait for official rollouts.
2. **Pattern Recognition:** What are early adopters in your field already doing? That's your future baseline.
3. **Scenario Building:** If this trend continues, what becomes possible? Build for that world.
4. **Rapid Experimentation:** Test weak signals before they become strong trends.

The only real barrier to change is your willingness to own the problem—and the future it represents.

THE DARK SIDE OF INFLUENCE

Here's where many people get trapped. They see these emerging futures, these possibilities on the horizon, and instead of claiming ownership, they look for an expert to follow. They search for the guru who's "figured it all out," the influencer with the perfect framework, the thought leader with tomorrow's answers today.

This is the opposite of horizon scanning. Horizon scanners look for weak signals and act on them. Guru followers wait for strong signals interpreted by someone else. In the age of AI, this difference becomes catastrophic.

The horizon scanner asks: "What's barely visible that might matter?"

The guru follower asks: "What's everyone else talking about?"

One question leads to the future; the other leads to the past disguised as the present.

Let me address something that keeps people stuck: the guru mindset. AI can provide instant information and even generate solutions, making expert knowledge potentially less valuable than the ability to ask better questions and adapt quickly. The guru dependency fosters precisely the wrong mindset in an era that rewards continuous learning over static expertise.

Think about it: if AI can access and synthesize all recorded human knowledge in seconds, what's the value of following someone who claims to have "the answers"? The future belongs to those who can ask better questions, not those who memorize someone else's answers.

So, basically, what do we tell people who are waiting for permission to start learning again? The cost of waiting for permission is higher than the cost of making mistakes. In the time you spend seeking approval or looking to link with some guru, someone else is already many learning cycles ahead of you.

As for the dark side of influencing, let's explore why this dependency is so dangerous in our accelerating world.

Dependency Creation Over Empowerment.

True gurus create followers who can't function without them. They become a bottleneck to growth and do not act as catalysts for change. In the AI era, this could be catastrophic. Followers need to become independent learners, not permanent disciples.

The Dependency Test: *The next time you're about to buy a course or follow a guru, ask, Will this teach me to fish, or will I need to keep coming back for fish? Watch for phrases like "my proprietary system" or "secret method." Real teachers make their methods transparent. Fake gurus make them mysterious.*

Example: *Remember how Finnish teachers are trusted to adapt methods to their students? They're not following a guru's playbook. They're using principles to create context-specific solutions. That's empowerment.*

The Attention Economy Addiction.

Social media has turned influence into performance metrics: likes, shares, followers. Gurus and influencers optimize for engagement over actual transformation. They say what gets reposted, not what creates lasting change or helps communities.

The 48-Hour Reality Check: *Take any viral business advice post with 100K+ likes. Apply it exactly as written for 48 hours and then document what actually happens. You'll quickly discover that what works in a caption rarely works in context. I tried "Rise and Grind at 4:00 a.m." By day three, I was too exhausted to think creatively. My best ideas come at 10:00 p.m. Your rhythm isn't their rhythm.*

Red Flag Signal: *When someone's advice could fit on a motivational poster, it's probably performance, not progress.*

Solution Selling Instead of Problem Solving.

The influencer gurus package most things, if not everything, into neat frameworks and courses. Real learning is messy, personal, and can't be commodified. When influence becomes about selling solutions rather than developing problem-solving capabilities, it can kill the very agency people need.

The Framework Trap: *"Seven Steps to..." "The Five Pillars of..." "The Ultimate Blueprint for..." Sound familiar? Here's what they don't tell you: Sugata Mitra didn't have a "Hole-in-the-Wall Framework." Sarah Blakely didn't follow "The Ten Commandments of Disruption." They encountered problems and found solutions. The framework came after the success, not before.*

Builder's Alternative: *Instead of buying another course, spend that money on materials or a subscription for a prototype. You'll learn more from one failed experiment than from ten perfect frameworks.*

The Wisdom Bypass.

Gurus often skip the struggle and present the polished outcome. This can rob followers of the essential experiences needed to work through difficult situations and build resilience—exactly what people need to thrive in uncertain times.

The Instagram Reality: *A guru posts a photo in their Manhattan penthouse with the caption "Started from the bottom." What they don't show: the trust fund, the connections, the twelve failed ventures funded by family. It's not because they're lying, but because struggle doesn't photograph well. Meanwhile, you're comparing your Chapter 2 to their Chapter 20.*

The Struggle Portfolio*: Document your failures like achievements. I keep a "Learning Log" of each mistake, what I learned from it, and how it shaped my next attempt. That portfolio is worth more than any certificate. As we learned in Chapter 4, fireflies flash and rest—the darkness between flashes isn't failure; it's regeneration.*

Scale Over Depth.

The pressure to influence at scale often results in generic advice that works for no one specifically. We often see this on platforms like Instagram and LinkedIn. Real transformation occurs through specific, contextualized guidance, which is largely the opposite of viral content.

***The Context Question**: Whenever you see advice like "This morning routine will change your life," ask, "For whom? A single parent in Mumbai? A farmer in Iowa? A night-shift nurse?" Generic advice assumes generic lives, but as we learned from Te Matua Ngahere, growth happens in specific soil, specific conditions, specific communities.*

***The One-Person Test**: Instead of creating content for thousands, solve one real person's specific problem completely. Document it. That case study will teach more than a hundred generic posts. Remember: Fireflies don't try to light the whole forest. They attract the right mates with the right signal.*

So, what's the firefly alternative? Instead of creating followers, fireflies create other leaders. They illuminate spaces where people discover their own light, rather than becoming dependent on external illumination. The question isn't how to influence more people. It's how to help people become more influential themselves.

THE GURU CHECKLIST:

- ☐ Do they share their failures as openly as their successes?
- ☐ Can you trace their advice to specific contexts and results?
- ☐ Do they teach principles you can adapt or rules you must follow?

- ☐ Are they creating independent thinkers or dependent followers?
- ☐ Would their advice work if they weren't there to interpret it?

If you answered "no" to any of these, you might be looking at performance, not progress. A guru, not a guide. An influencer, not an igniter.

Very few can light your glow but you.

BREAKING THE GURU CODE

The influencer gurus package most things, if not everything, into neat frameworks and courses. Real learning is messy and personal and can't be commodified. When influence becomes about selling solutions rather than developing problem-solving capabilities, it can kill the very agency people need.

THE FRAMEWORK TRAP:

- "Seven Steps to..."
- "The Five Pillars of…"
- "The Ultimate Blueprint for…"
- "Most people have X but aren't using it to its potential…"

Sound familiar? Here's what they don't tell you: As we discussed previously, Sarah Blakely didn't follow "The Ten Commandments of Disruption."

She founded Spanx and built a multi-million-dollar, if not billion-dollar, company by taking complete ownership of both the problem and the solution.

When she was selling fax machines door to door and cutting the feet off her pantyhose, she wasn't executing some guru's "Disruptive Innovation Playbook." No MBA. No fashion degree. No "How to

Build a Billion-Dollar Brand" course. Just scissors, determination, and a problem that bothered her enough to solve it.

Spanx became a revolutionary shapewear company that transformed the undergarment industry. She started with five thousand dollars of her own savings, no investors, no fashion experience—just a problem she wanted to solve (looking good in white pants without visible panty lines).

And here's another one: Ron Finley, the "Gangsta Gardener" of South LA, didn't have a masterclass on "Urban Food Revolution in Ten Easy Steps." He saw his community—a food desert with plenty of liquor stores but no fresh produce—and started planting vegetables in abandoned lots and street medians. No permission. No framework. Just dirt under his fingernails and a vision.[80]

When the city cited him for gardening without permits, he didn't consult a guru or buy a course on "Municipal Navigation for Rebels." He fought back and kept planting, declaring, "Growing your own food is like printing your own money." His TED talk has over four million views, but more importantly, he sparked a global guerrilla gardening movement. City policies changed, and communities transformed, all because one person decided to own a problem instead of waiting for a solution.[81]

And speaking of ownership without permission—remember Howard Schultz and the café latte example from earlier? Well, lightning struck twice. Dina Campion, a Starbucks manager in California, noticed customers in the summer heat looking longingly at hot coffee but walking away. She didn't wait for Seattle headquarters to develop a cold beverage strategy. Instead, she started experimenting with blended coffee drinks in her store.[82]

Corporate's response? "Starbucks doesn't do blended drinks. We're a coffee company, not a smoothie shop." But Campion had something frameworks don't provide—actual customers wanting to buy her creation. She kept making them, kept tracking sales, kept building evidence. The

Frappuccino now generates over two billion dollars in annual revenue. That's billion with a "b." From one manager who didn't wait for the "Official Beverage Innovation Framework."[83]

They encountered problems and found solutions. The frameworks came after the success, not before.

TRANSFORMATION STORIES

Real ownership looks different from what most imagine. Take Ron Finley's deeper story—when the city gave him a citation that was turning into a warrant for his parkway garden, he didn't just resist. He said, "Cool. Bring it." The LA Times picked it up, 900 people signed a petition on Change.org, and suddenly, his councilman was calling to endorse what he was doing. But here's what matters: Finley wasn't just planting vegetables. As he puts it, "Gardening is my graffiti. I grow my art." When that mother and daughter showed up at 10:30 at night looking for food, looking ashamed, he told them: 'You don't have to do this like this. This is on the street for a reason. That's ownership—not just solving your own problem, but creating solutions that transform shame into dignity, one garden at a time.

This pattern of ownership ripples globally. At India's Barefoot College, rural women who never attended school now build and maintain solar installations across their villages, succeeding where top-down electrification failed. They didn't wait for government infrastructure; they became the infrastructure.

In New Zealand, Ngāti Whātua Ōrākei—descendants of the rangatira Tuperiri who have maintained ahi kā (unbroken occupation) since the seventeenth century—plan generations ahead for their seven thousand hapū members worldwide. As tangata whenua of Tāmaki, they don't wait for government vision; their Trust weaves ancestral wisdom with modern governance, taking responsibility for their mokopuna's (grandchildren's) futures today.

Sometimes the spark comes from unexpected places. After Mexico City's devastating earthquakes, residents created their own neighborhood warning and response networks rather than waiting for official systems. In Medellín, Colombia, communities transformed their city through innovative transit solutions that connected isolated neighborhoods to opportunity. When Comuna 13's residents gained their famous orange escalators, replacing a twenty-eight-story daily climb with a six-minute ride, they didn't just get better transportation—they reclaimed ownership of their neighborhood. As architect Carlos Escobar noted, "The control is in the community's hands."

Not every story succeeds. Detroit's urban farming movement shows both promise and pitfalls—some lots flourish while others fail, teaching us that ownership requires more than good intentions. But from community-driven health insurance in Rwanda to fishing communities who blend traditional weather knowledge with modern forecasting, ownership isn't about having resources—it's about claiming problems as yours to solve.

THE FEAR BEHIND THE PERMISSION

Here's what no one talks about: The permission addiction isn't just laziness or lack of initiative. **It's fear**.

Here's the truth: Fear of ownership is perfectly rational. This fear, pure and distilled, often masquerades as prudence.

When you wait for permission, failure belongs to the system. When you take ownership, failure has your name on it. That's uncomfortable, but it's also where the magic lives.

The Fear Inventory

Let's name the fears that keep us seeking permission:

- **Fear of visibility:** When you take ownership, you can't hide in the crowd anymore. Your work, your decisions, your mistakes—

all visible. As one teacher told me, "If I just follow the curriculum, no one can blame me. If I innovate and students fail, that's on me."

- **Fear of inadequacy:** "What if I'm not expert enough?" This fear whispers that you need one more course, one more certification, one more year of experience.
- **Fear of resources:** "I don't have what they had." This fear highlights every advantage others possess that you lack.
- **Fear of irreversibility:** "What if I burn bridges?" This fear imagines that taking ownership means destroying all other options. It pictures dramatic exits and slammed doors, not realizing that most ownership starts quietly, experimentally, and reversibly.

The Firefly Response to Fear

But here's what I learned from studying fireflies: they flash despite predators. Every time a firefly lights up, it risks being eaten, yet it flashes anyway. Why? **Because not flashing guarantees genetic death.** No light, no mates, no future.

Your situation is similar. Not taking ownership guarantees professional and creative death, just slower and less dramatic. You'll wake up in ten years having built nothing, changed nothing, and owned nothing. That should scare you more than any failure.

The Fear Transformation Toolkit

So, how do we transform fear from a barrier into fuel?

- **Start with reversible experiments:** Your first ownership move doesn't have to be quitting your job or revolutionizing your industry.
- **Document everything:** Fear hates data. Keep a simple log: *"Tried X, resulted in Y, learned Z."* When fear says, "Everything you

touch fails," your log says, "Actually, seven out of ten experiments taught me something valuable."

- **Find your "fear buddy":** This shouldn't be a cheerleader who says everything will be fine, but someone who's also taking ownership and facing fear. Text each other your small wins and spectacular failures. Fear loses power when it's shared.
- **Reframe failure as tuition:** Every mistake is education you paid for. I've never met a successful builder who didn't have a collection of expensive lessons. The only waste is not learning from them.

THE 48-HOUR FEAR TEST

Here's an exercise that changed my relationship with fear, told to me by a former colleague. First, write down the worst thing that can happen from your best idea. Be specific. *"If I propose this solution and it fails, then..."*

Now live with that scenario for 48 hours. Don't fight it. Let it sit there. You'll notice something interesting: The fear peaks in the first few hours and then starts to fade. By day two, your brain starts solving for the worst case: *If that happened, I could... and then I'd probably...*

Fear thrives on vagueness. Specificity kills it.

THE OTHER SIDE OF FEAR

Remember in Chapter 4 when we talked about fireflies flashing and resting? Fear is part of the cycle. It's not a bug in the system—it's a feature. Fear means you're attempting something that matters.

The question isn't "How do I eliminate fear?" It's "How do I act despite fear?"

Here's what waits on the other side: A teacher we met as part of the data gathering for this book used to be terrified of diverging from the curriculum. Now she runs professional development workshops on innovation.

She didn't overcome fear. She learned to dance with it.

Your fear is not a stop sign.

It's a signal that you're about to do something that matters.

Something that could change everything.

Something that deserves to have your name on it.

So, yes, taking ownership is terrifying. Do it anyway. Your future self is counting on it.

YOUR FIRST CHESS MOVE

Right now, I want you to identify your first chess move—not your master plan, not your perfect strategy, but your first move that creates forward momentum.

As I mentioned at my TEDx talk in Shanghai, even transformative projects start simply: "It was my first chess move." However, the initial skeletal structure can become something that reshapes how people think about learning forever.

What's one problem in your sphere of influence that you can claim ownership of this week? Not solve completely, not transform entirely, just claim and start.

Maybe it's a learning challenge in your classroom. Maybe it's a communication breakdown in your team. Maybe it's a community need that everyone complains about but no one addresses.

We need to stop thinking like consultants who analyze every problem. Then we need to start thinking like owners who actually solve problems.

We can use modern technology to research solutions. We can use digital platforms to connect with others facing similar challenges, employ prototyping tools to test approaches quickly, and activate our Builder's Backpack to move from idea to implementation.

But start today with what you have, where you are, because the moment you make that first move, something shifts. The problem becomes yours. The energy changes. Resources you didn't know existed appear. People who were waiting for someone to lead suddenly want to help.

Here's what makes this moment in history unique and the first chess move more democratized than ever: The tools for building have never been more accessible. AI can help you research in minutes what used to take weeks. No-code platforms let you build applications without programming knowledge. Global communities mean you can find collaborators across continents. Online learning means you can acquire skills on demand.

The old excuses—"I don't have the resources," "I don't have the expertise," "I don't have the connections"—are evaporating. What's left is the real barrier: ownership.

Will you claim the problem as yours to solve?

30-DAY OWNERSHIP SPRINT

The 30-Day Ownership Sprint begins with a public declaration. Not private journaling—public commitment. Post on it somewhere, tell your team, or email your most judgmental friend: "I'm taking ownership of [specific problem] and will have [specific deliverable] by [date thirty days from now]."

Week 1 (Days 1–7): Problem Immersion.

Live with the problem you're solving. If there's a communication breakdown in your team, document every painful instance. If it's inefficient learning systems, experience the inefficiency viscerally. No solutions yet—just deep understanding. Create a "Problem Journal" and share it with an accountability partner, who asks daily, "What did you observe today?" By Day 7, you should hate the problem so much that not solving it feels unbearable.

Week 2 (Days 8–14): Solution Prototyping.

Build three different solutions—intentionally different approaches. Use AI to accelerate—have Claude design solution architectures, use ChatGPT to identify similar problems solved elsewhere, and use Perplexity to research tools. But build with your hands. Ugly is fine; non-existent is not. Share all three prototypes with five people experiencing the problem by Day 14.

Week 3 (Days 15–21): Iteration Based on Reality.

Take feedback, pick the most promising direction, and rebuild. This week separates builders from dreamers—when real users critique your baby, will you defend it or improve it? Document what you're learning; these insights matter more than the solution. By Day 21, have version 2.0, which incorporates actual user feedback.

Week 4 (Days 22–30): Launch and Measure.

Ship something real. Not perfect—real. If it's a new team communication system, implement it. If it's a learning tool, have five people use it. Measure one metric that matters—time saved, problems solved, stress reduced.

Day 30: Public report.

Share what you built, what worked, what failed, what you learned. The cycle is complete; you're now addicted to ownership. You'll claim the next problem without needing a framework.

Weave in the Firefly Wheel to check and balance each of your stages.

THE COMPOUND EFFECT OF OWNERSHIP

When you take ownership, something remarkable happens: It compounds.

Your first project might be small—maybe you solve a scheduling problem for your team using simple automation—but that success builds confidence. You tackle something bigger. Others notice. They want to learn. Suddenly, you're not just solving problems; you're creating problem solvers.

I've watched this happen countless times. A teacher who starts by creating better worksheets with AI ends up transforming their entire class's approach to personalized learning. A manager who builds a simple dashboard to track team performance ends up revolutionizing how their company thinks about data.

Consider Lou Groen and the Filet-O-Fish. He didn't set out to create a global menu item generating hundreds of millions of dollars annually. He just wanted to solve his Friday sales problem. But ownership compounds. His single sandwich solution became a template for local innovation across the entire McDonald's system.

Or think about Ken Kutaragi and the PlayStation. His "side project" of developing a sound chip—which Sony leadership actively opposed—didn't just become a gaming console. It transformed Sony's entire identity and created a twenty-five billion dollar division. One engineer's ownership became an industry transformation.

The first chess move might seem insignificant, but ownership compounds. Each problem you solve makes you capable of solving bigger problems. Each person you inspire creates more capacity for change.

THE FUTURE BELONGS TO BUILDERS

We're preparing for a future where the old hierarchies dissolve into dynamic communities. Where AI handles routine thinking so humans can focus on the unprecedented. Where the ability to spot problems and build solutions matters more than your title or tenure.

Consider how the builders of our time embody this shift. When Ray Dalio started Bridgewater Associates from his two-bedroom apartment in 1975, he didn't wait for Wall Street's permission to reimagine investment. He built a system of "radical transparency" and "idea meritocracy" that challenged every hierarchical norm of finance. His principle: the best idea wins, regardless of who it comes from. Today, Bridgewater manages $150 billion by operating more like a dynamic community than a traditional hierarchy.[84]

Or look at how builders approach AI itself. While others debate whether AI will replace jobs, Elon Musk asks different questions: How do we merge with it? How do we ensure it serves humanity? He doesn't wait for regulations or consensus. SpaceX uses AI to land rockets. Tesla's autopilot learns from every mile driven. Neuralink explores brain-computer interfaces. Right or wrong, he builds toward the future he envisions.[85]

Steve Jobs understood this perhaps better than anyone. "It's better to be a pirate than join the navy," he told the original Macintosh team.[86] When he returned to Apple in 1997, he didn't seek the board's permission for every decision. He killed dozens of products, simplified everything, and built what he believed people needed before they knew they needed it. No focus groups. No permission slips. Just conviction turned into products.

Mark Zuckerberg's Harvard dorm room project perfectly illustrates ownership scaling. He didn't wait for university approval to connect students online. He built Facebook in a weekend and tested it on classmates, and when Harvard tried to shut it down, he expanded to other schools. Today, whether you love or hate what Facebook has become, you can't deny the ownership mindset that created it: See the problem, build a solution, scale what works.[87]

In this future, the permission seekers will be left behind, not because they lack talent or intelligence, but because they're waiting for a starting gun that will never fire. They're seeking approval from systems that are themselves becoming obsolete.

Meanwhile, the builders—the ones who see problems and claim them, who start with what they have, who measure progress not perfection—are creating the future one project at a time.

YOUR OWNERSHIP DECLARATION

As we close this chapter, I want you to make a declaration. Not to me, not to your boss, not to anyone else. To yourself.

Complete this sentence: **"I am going to take ownership of ____________ and I'm going to start by ____________."**

Be specific. Be realistic. But most importantly, be committed.

Once you understand the power of ownership, once you've tasted what it feels like to stop waiting and start building, the next question becomes, How do you build systematically? How do you turn initial momentum into lasting transformation?

That's where the real building begins.

The permission slip you've been waiting for? You're holding it. You've always been holding it.

It's time to use it.

CHAPTER 8

BEYOND REIMAGINATION: TIME TO BUILD

"The funny thing about sustainability, you have to sustain it."

— Ron Finley

Signal from the Future: *The Department of Future Housing releases another five-hundred-page report on the homeless crisis, projecting that solutions won't be implemented until 2040. Three teenagers use AI and salvaged materials to 3D-print a full shelter community over spring break. The department schedules a meeting to discuss whether the shelters violate zoning laws.*

I gave a colleague who teaches in New York the *Firefly Wheel* three months ago, and he tested it with his most challenging class. Instead of teaching predetermined content, he asked students, within the structure of a real scenario, to identify problems in their community they wanted to solve. One group tackled fresh food deserts, another addressed youth violence, and a third designed better bus routes. He used AI tools to help them research, prototype, and test solutions.

Standardized test scores? Irrelevant. What matters: Three students simply started a project driven by passion and purpose, engagement soared, and the student everyone had written off became one of the lead presenters. His reflection captured it perfectly: "I finally understand—we don't need to always be teaching students content. We need to teach them to build."

The momentum is spreading. Readers of early drafts are forming "builder circles"—weekly meetups where people share what they're creating. No presentations or theory, just people showing work in progress and helping each other solve problems.

In a virtual vision circle last week. A teacher gathered feedback on her AI-enhanced lesson plans. An engineer demonstrated an early demo of his health tracking application, and a marketing executive shared her community micro-learning platform. Each person had ten minutes to show their build and gather feedback.

What struck me most was their shared philosophy: "Starting is the hardest part. After that, momentum takes over." Every builder told the same story—they had previously felt frustrated by a routine of waiting for perfect conditions but this environment had allowed them to own the problem, create something gritty that barely worked, gave them a pathway to keep improving it, and most were growing in confidence that eventually they would hit a product breakthrough. Not one person had "enough" resources or the "right" credentials. They just started building.

That's the pattern: Stop waiting for permission. Start building solutions.

THE BUILDING IMPERATIVE

We've spent enough time reimagining.

In Chapter 7, you identified your first chess move. You claimed ownership of a problem. You saw how builders like Sarah Blakely, Lou Groen, and Sugata Mitra turned ownership into reality. Now it's time for you to join them.

Most "innovation" is intellectual kayfabe.

You're getting off on planning while your competitors are getting rich by building. Every day you spend in another reimagination meeting is another day closer to irrelevance. They create beautiful presentations, decks, and blueprints about what could be. They hold endless meetings about what should be. They detail strategies about what might be.

Building means putting something real into the world that didn't exist before, something you can touch, test, and improve, something that solves actual problems for actual people.

In a world where AI can turn your rough ideas into polished prototypes in minutes, where global collaboration platforms connect you instantly with experts, where automation handles routine tasks so you can focus on creation, the question isn't whether you can build.

The question is: What are you going to build, and how fast can you get started?

While you're still reimagining, someone else is building. And they're going to win.

WHY REIMAGINATION IS SEDUCTIVE (BUT INSUFFICIENT)

Let me tell you why so many people get stuck in the reimagination loop. In my experience leading teams across continents, reimagination is a safe space. It's safe because you rarely have to put anything in front of the people who matter.

I've worked with teams who love the reimagination process, and they will stay in it as long as possible. Why? Because, ultimately, when you have a solution, you have to put it in front of a key stakeholder—and it could be rejected.

I get it. It's scary. There's a vulnerability in real innovation that reimagination doesn't require.

When you reimagine, you're playing with possibilities. When you build, you're committing to reality. Reimagination feels productive—look at all these ideas! Building feels risky—what if this doesn't work?

But here's the firefly truth: Each failure is dimming before a brighter burst. As we explored in Chapter 4, fireflies don't glow continuously. They flash, rest, learn, and flash brighter. Your first build might be dim. Your second will be brighter. But you'll never glow at all if you stay in the planning phase.

THE STRATEGIC BUILDING PROCESS

Let me give you the methodology for turning ideas into reality. This is the process I've used to help build innovative schools across the world, and it works for any domain—corporate, educational, or community.

Phase One: The Vision Lock.

Not a mission statement or strategic plan, but a crystal-clear picture of the specific problem you're solving and the outcome you're creating. You need to be able to explain it in one sentence to anybody—the elevator pitch.

For example: "We're designing systems where questions matter more than answers."

Simple. Measurable. Memorable.

Remember, you need to study and appreciate empathy here. You need empathy for the people you're building for. As we learned from Chapter 6, true innovation honors the human element.

Phase Two: Battle Selection.

Here's the crucial insight: You can't fight every battle. Successful builders pick their fights strategically.

When do you fight?

- When the problem directly blocks your vision.
- When you have unique insight or capability.
- When winning creates momentum for bigger battles.
- When the cost of not fighting exceeds the cost of fighting.

When do you avoid the fight?

- When it's someone else's core responsibility.
- When victory doesn't advance your main objective.
- When you lack the resources to win decisively.
- When the battle distracts from higher-priority work.

This isn't about avoiding conflict—it's about strategic focus. Every battle you choose not to fight gives you more energy for the battles that matter.

Phase Three: The Alliance Strategy.

Early stages: Design alone but validate constantly. Your vision needs to be authentically yours, but it also needs to solve real problems for real people.

Key growth stages:

- **Recruit selectively:** Hire slow, fire fast. It sounds harsh, but it's crucial. Use technology to generate candidate profiles and assessment criteria, but trust your instincts for cultural fit.

- **Scale systematically:** Build systems, not just teams. The goal isn't to create dependency on you as founder—it's to create capability that outlasts you.

Phase Four: Technology Leverage.

Here's where it gets interesting. Technology and digital tools aren't just helpful for building—they're revolutionary.

AI can:

- Generate business plans in minutes.
- Create prototypes from descriptions.
- Analyze market research instantly.
- Draft communications.
- Design workflows.
- Solve technical problems.

But—and this is crucial—technology amplifies your vision and accelerates your execution. It doesn't replace your judgment or act as a substitute for your leadership.

THE BUILDING ACCELERATORS

Let me show you how modern tools can accelerate every phase of building:

- **Vision Development:** Use AI to analyze thousands of similar projects and identify patterns. Most AI systems now have deep research features. Feed it your rough ideas and ask for variations, challenges, and improvements, but the final vision lock still depends on your human insight.

- **Market Research:** Leverage AI's deep research capabilities instead of spending months on surveys and focus groups. Tools like Claude's research mode can analyze thousands of sources simultaneously, Perplexity can track real-time market sentiment, and ChatGPT can identify patterns across industries. These systems can now read academic papers, synthesize competitor strategies, and surface weak signals from social conversations—delivering insights in hours that previously took quarters to compile.
- **Prototype Creation:** No-code platforms let you build functional versions without programming. 3D printing makes physical prototypes more accessible than ever. AI can generate initial designs, content, and even code. The barrier between idea and prototype has essentially disappeared. We are in a completely new frontier. My advice: embrace this.
- **Team Building:** Use digital platforms to find collaborators globally: LinkedIn for professional networking, Discord for community building, and Slack for team coordination. Geography is no longer a constraint on talent.
- **Testing and Iteration:** Digital analytics give real-time feedback on what's working. A/B testing platforms let you compare approaches scientifically. AI can analyze user behavior patterns and suggest improvements. AI can take you deeper than ever before—analyzing your user feedback and identifying hidden patterns, and acting like an experienced consultant who looks at how people use your website or product and suggests practical improvements.

Here's the key: All these tools require human judgment to use effectively. They make good builders better. They can't make non-builders into builders.

THE BOTTLENECK REALITY

The bottleneck isn't tools or resources anymore, so we can't blame them. The bottleneck is decision-making—the speed and courage of decision-makers.

This connects to a fundamental firefly principle: flash or fade. Fireflies that hesitate to flash don't mate. They don't pass on their genes. They disappear from the gene pool entirely. Nature doesn't reward the firefly that waits for perfect darkness or ideal weather conditions. It rewards the one that flashes when the moment arrives.

The same law applies to builders. While you're analyzing options, someone somewhere is testing solutions. While you're waiting for the perfect moment to flash, another firefly is already attracting partners, already creating the next generation.

Think about it. In nature, the pause between decision and action can mean extinction. In our accelerated world, the gap between idea and implementation determines who shapes the future and who gets shaped by it.

The tools are democratized. The resources are accessible. The only scarce resource left is the courage to flash—to make decisions quickly, test rapidly, and learn immediately. That's why we see young builders like Vitalik Buterin—just nineteen when he wrote the white paper that would become Ethereum—perfectly representing the collapse of time we discussed in Chapter 1.

The bottleneck has moved from the external to the internal, from "Can we?" to "Will we?" and from capability to courage.

Flash or fade. Build or be built around. The choice—and the bottleneck—is yours.

REAL BUILDERS IN ACTION

Let's look at what systematic building looks like in practice—builders who went beyond reimagination:

Drew Houston – Dropbox:

Frustrated by constantly forgetting his USB drive, Drew didn't just complain about file-syncing problems. He built a solution, starting with a simple demo video showing files automatically syncing across devices. Posted to Hacker News, the video drove his beta waiting list from 5,000 to 75,000 users, validating demand before the full product launch.[88]

He chose his battles carefully, focusing only on seamless syncing and ignoring feature requests that didn't serve his core vision. Dropbox became a multi-billion-dollar company, built by focusing on one problem.

Sal Khan – Khan Academy:

Sal was an investment analyst who started making math videos to help his cousin with homework. When other family members asked for help, he put videos on YouTube instead of tutoring everyone individually. He built his platform incrementally, starting with one video, then ten, and eventually hundreds.

Sal quit his hedge fund job only after proving the concept. He chose to fight the battle for free, with accessible education rather than competing on premium features. As a result, he created the world's largest free learning platform, proving that systematic building around a core mission can transform entire industries.[89]

Tara Brach – Meditation Teacher:

Tara, a clinical psychologist, recognized that traditional therapy wasn't fully addressing spiritual suffering. She began leading small meditation groups, starting with intimate gatherings that grew organically as people experienced genuine transformation.

When demand increased, she developed systems, including online courses, teacher training, and community structures that could scale without compromising personal connection. Now she teaches hundreds of thousands globally, bridging ancient Buddhist wisdom with modern psychology.[90]

Notice the pattern? These builders didn't wait for perfect conditions or official approval. They:

- Saw problems and claimed ownership.
- Built solutions using available tools.
- Started small and proved value.
- Scaled systematically.
- Collaborated when it accelerated progress.
- Worked independently when collaboration slowed them down.

They understood something crucial: In our rapidly changing world, the most dangerous thing is waiting for the perfect moment to start building.

The perfect moment is now, with imperfect tools and incomplete information.

THE UGLY BABY PRINCIPLE

Here's a psychological barrier to building that no one talks about: perfectionism. Your first build will usually be ugly—embarrassingly ugly.

I know this personally. Starting out as an education leader, I recall mistakes I made regarding timetables, staff training, and reports. Five years later, you wouldn't recognize the school I led. I've lived through the ugly baby principle; it's an essential part of the growth.

But here's what matters: An ugly working prototype beats a beautiful plan every time. People can use ugly. They can give feedback on ugly. They can help you improve ugly. They can't do anything with perfect plans that don't exist.

The most important thing about learning is to flash. Nothing else matters except lighting up every day and trying.

THE 72-HOUR RULE

If you can't build a testable version of your idea within 72 hours, your idea is too big or too vague. Break it down until you can ship something—even if it's just:

- A landing page.
- A single feature.
- A hand-drawn prototype.

I do this constantly with my students. Just draw it. Just create. Launch something.

FIREFLY FLASHPOINT

Your first attempt will embarrass you.
Good. You're building while they're planning.

BUILD FOR THE DESPERATE

Before building anything, find someone experiencing the exact problem you want to solve. Observe them struggle with current solutions.

This principle led directly to Almach.ai, the artificial intelligence company we're launching now. It emerged from watching schools wrestle with learning management systems—a multi-billion-dollar industry that should deliver exceptional tools but instead leaves educators frustrated and underserved.

We've lived through an entire six-month firefly cycle building Almach, moving from observation to prototype to working solution. The difference? We built for desperate users who needed real help, not theoretical ones who might appreciate marginal improvements.

If people aren't actively seeking alternatives or paying money to solve the problem, don't build it. Build for those whose current pain makes them grateful for any genuine solution.

THE SCALING MOMENT

You can design alone, but you can't scale alone. The moment your solution starts working, you'll hit bottlenecks that you can't solve yourself. That's not failure—that's success demanding growth.

Plan for the moment when your individual ownership needs to become team ownership.

YOUR BUILDING ASSIGNMENT

Here's your assignment. Not a suggestion—an assignment.

Before you move to the next chapter, declare what you're building. Not what you're thinking about building, not what you might build someday, but what you're actually building, starting this week.

Set a deadline for your first working prototype. Not a perfect version, not a complete solution, but something that demonstrates your core concept. It could be a solution for you, your child, your friend, or your community.

Give it a month maximum. If you can't build a testable version within that time using available tools, your idea is too big or too vague.

Use AI to accelerate research and planning. Use digital platforms to find collaborators and early users. Use prototyping tools to make ideas tangible. Use the battle selection framework to focus strategically.

But build. Don't just plan to build. Don't just talk about building. Build something real that solves a real problem for real people.

THE VELOCITY ADVANTAGE

The numbers tell a story that reimagination alone never could. When Walmart faced the challenge of upskilling over a million employees for a digital future, they didn't just announce another training initiative—they built Live Better U. With over 126,000 associates participating and $730 million saved in tuition costs, they've created real pathways from frontline roles to careers in data analytics, software engineering, and supply chain management.[91]

The program offers everything from high school completion to bachelor's degrees in computer science, available to all associates from day one—no strings attached, no obligation to stay. What started as an experiment has become the model other retailers desperately try to copy. They didn't wait for the perfect program; they built, learned, and scaled. Now they're preparing to fill one hundred thousand new roles in the next three years, proving that building beats planning every time.

Scale amplifies these victories. A Fortune 100 food company's digital hub returned two million hours to three hundred thousand employees, not through automation but through intelligent augmentation. Employees designed the solutions, AI accelerated the implementation, and the metric that mattered wasn't technology adoption but human hours reclaimed for creative work.

Johnson & Johnson's cross-functional revolution produced similar results, with measurable outcomes in HR decision science that traditional approaches never achieved. But perhaps most instructive is TikTok's trajectory—building a sixteen billion dollar advertising empire in five years while established media companies held strategy meetings. They didn't have better plans. They had better building velocity.

The pattern holds across domains. Midjourney evolved from version one to six in two years, with each iteration based on user feedback rather than committee decisions. Nigeria created the first approved subnational social protection laws not through endless policy papers but through pilot programs that demonstrated what worked. Even LEGO's transformation from near-bankruptcy to global dominance came not from strategic brilliance but from systematic building—testing product lines, killing what failed, and doubling down on what succeeded. Microsoft's Azure transformation under Satya Nadella followed the same principle: build, measure, learn, repeat.

The six-month cycles we advocate aren't just theory—companies using them report productivity gains that five-year plans never delivered. The evidence is overwhelming: In an age of AI acceleration, the builders inherit the earth while the planners inherit PowerPoints.

THE FIREFLY BUILDER'S TRUTH

Once you start building systematically, you'll discover something amazing: The act of creation generates more energy and insight than any amount of planning ever could.

Remember from Chapter 4: Fireflies generate their own light through action, not intention. The chemical reaction happens when elements combine. Your creative light happens when ideas meet reality.

But how do you sustain that creative energy over the long term? How do you keep your explorer's spirit alive when building gets hard and obstacles multiply?

That's where real mastery begins.

THE REGENERATIVE MOMENT: FROM VISION TO VERSION

Before you rush to the next chapter, before you close this book to "think about it later," stop. This is your regenerative moment—the pause between planning and doing where real builders separate from eternal dreamers.

Four Questions to Ignite Your Build:

1. **What's the smallest version of your idea that would prove it works?**

   Not the grand vision. Not the five-year plan. The tiny, testable kernel that demonstrates your core concept. Sarah Blakely, founder of Spanx, started with one pair of pantyhose and a pair of scissors, cutting the feet off to create a smoother look under white pants. Sal Khan, founder of Khan Academy, started with one math video for his cousin. What's your equivalent? Strip away every feature except the one that matters. That's your starting point.

2. **Who is desperately seeking a solution to the problem you want to solve?**

   Not who might theoretically benefit. Who is actively struggling, searching, maybe even paying for inferior solutions right now? These are your first users, your validators, your co-creators. Find one person—just one—who needs what you're building. Their feedback is worth more than a thousand focus groups.

3. **Where have you seen failure become a turning point, not a dead end?**

   Think back to your own journey or one you've witnessed. When did a spectacular failure lead to unexpected insight? When did a closed door reveal a better path? Your building journey will include failures. Knowing they're turning points, not endpoints, changes everything. Write down one failure that led to a breakthrough. Keep it visible as you build.

4. **What's your process for turning ideas into form?**

   Whether it's a curriculum, company, or culture, how do you personally move from thought to thing? Some people sketch. Others prototype.

Some talk the idea through until it crystallizes. What's your way? If you don't know, experiment this week. Try three different methods. Find what makes ideas flow into form for you.

THE 48-HOUR CHALLENGE

Here's my challenge: Within forty-eight hours of reading this, create something tangible related to your idea. Anything. A sketch on a napkin. A one-page outline. A conversation with a potential user. A domain name. A rough prototype.

Why forty-eight hours? Because after that, the urgency fades. The reimagination loop calls you back. The comfortable fog of "someday" rolls in.

Remember the firefly insight from Chapter 4: Each flash is both an ending and a beginning. This regenerative moment is your flash—the pause between consuming ideas and creating reality.

Your move.

CHAPTER 9

KEEPING THE EXPLORER ALIVE: SUSTAINING CURIOSITY IN A CHANGING WORLD

"The cure for boredom is curiosity.
There is no cure for curiosity."

— Dorothy Parker

Signal from the Future: *A doctor, once one of the world's leading cancer researchers, watches his forty years of expertise get replicated by AI in nanoseconds. Instead of retiring bitter, he teaches young doctors what AI can't: how to help a terrified patient prepare for treatment. When to lean forward, when to slow down, how to say, "You're going to get through this" in a way that quiets the panic. He becomes more essential than ever.*

THE CURIOSITY CRISIS

Here's the thing nobody tells you about building and creating: It can kill your curiosity if you're not careful.

The pressure to deliver results, to scale effectively, to optimize processes can turn explorers into operators and fireflies into factory lights. Eventually, you start executing instead of experimenting, managing instead of discovering.

I've spent years working with brilliant innovators and watching them become bureaucrats of their own creations. It's terribly sad. Teachers who revolutionized learning environments get promoted to administrators and begin standardizing everything they once disrupted. Entrepreneurs who shattered industries become executives more concerned with protecting market share than remaining changemakers.

The very success of building can extinguish the explorer's spirit that made building possible in the first place.

Here's what's at stake. We're entering an era where the half-life of skills continues to collapse, where AI reshapes entire industries overnight, and where the fusion of human creativity with technological capability creates infinite possibilities. In this world, your ability to stay curious—to keep exploring, questioning, and experimenting—isn't just personally fulfilling; it's professionally essential and culturally critical.

The future belongs to lifelong explorers who never stop lighting their spark for learning.

BUILDING THE EXPLORER'S OPERATING SYSTEM

Let me provide you with a framework for maintaining curiosity throughout your life, regardless of how successful or busy you become.

THE FIREFLY REGENERATIVE CYCLE

Remember: Fireflies don't glow constantly. They flash intensely, then rest, then flash brighter. This isn't just energy management—it's curiosity maintenance.

The cycle works like this:

Phase One: Intense Exploration (two months).

Pick one area you know nothing about but are genuinely curious to understand—not because it's useful for work, not because it's trending, but because it sparks genuine wonder in you.

Use AI to quickly map the landscape. What are the core concepts? Who are the key thinkers? What are the unsolved problems? Get oriented fast; then dive deep into what intrigues you most.

Phase Two: Creative Integration (two months).

Now the magic happens. How does this new knowledge connect with what you already know? What unexpected patterns emerge? What novel combinations become possible?

I've made a career out of this—teaching interdisciplinary, project-based learning. There's incredible reward in mixing what traditional education calls siloed domains. Weird and wonderful combinations create the most incredible prototypes. A student who combined marine biology with architecture designed floating cities. Another, who merged music theory with data science, created algorithms that compose symphonies.

Phase Three: Experimental Application (two months).

Build something small that applies your integrated insights. Test whether your new understanding actually works in the real world. Share it with others.

This isn't about creating perfection. It's about staying connected to the creative process.

THE CURIOSITY MAINTENANCE SYSTEM

Daily Micro-Explorations:

What might happen if you spent fifteen minutes every day engaging with something unrelated to your professional responsibilities? Read poetry if you're an engineer. Study finance if you're an artist. Explore mycology if you work in education.

Use AI to suggest connections between disparate fields. Let technology help you discover what you didn't know you wanted to learn.

This follows the firefly principle of compound illumination: each small flash of learning connects to create larger patterns of understanding.

Weekly Wonder Sessions:

Once a week, engage in pure play. No objectives. No outcomes. No optimization. Build something useless. Explore somewhere new. Have conversations with people outside your usual circles.

This isn't frivolous—it's essential. Play is where innovation incubates. Wonder is where breakthrough insights emerge.

Monthly Perspective Shifts:

Once a month, dramatically change your environment. Visit a different neighborhood. Attend an event outside your expertise. Spend time with people from different generations or cultures.

For over ten years, I did this as a job. Every three months, I would dramatically change my environment—from the Sacred Valley in Peru to the hustle of Mumbai, from the solemn Atomic Bomb Dome of Hiroshima to the thunder of Iguazu Falls.

It's hard to feel the plateau when you're swept up in Mumbai's Ganesh Festival, hard to feel stuck when standing before the Burj Khalifa—so tall it experiences different weather at its base and summit—and hard to feel uninspired at the gates of Machu Picchu.

Your perspective can be your prison if you don't regularly escape it.

Quarterly Assumption Challenges:

Every quarter, choose one assumption underlying your work and challenge it systematically. What if the opposite were true? What if the constraints were removed? What if the problem were redefined entirely?

This prevents the crystallization of thinking that turns explorers into operators.

THE SIX-MONTH FIREFLY PLAN

The Six-Month Firefly Plan I'm about to share integrates directly with the Firefly Wheel from Chapter 4. While the Wheel gives you the framework for any learning cycle, this plan provides the specific timeline and milestones for sustained implementation. Think of the Wheel as your compass and the Six-Month Plan as your map.

Spark (Week 1)

- Identify what's bothering you enough to act
- Build the smallest possible solution
- Share it immediately, however rough

Flash (Months 1-2)

- Rapid iterations based on real feedback
- Use AI to accelerate research and prototyping
- Connect with others solving similar problems
- Build, test, adjust - in days, not months

Converge (Months 3-4)

- Your solution attracts collaborators
- Patterns emerge from actual use
- Unexpected applications appear
- Community forms around the work

Glow (Month 5)

- Sustained impact becomes visible
- Others adapt and improve your work
- New problems reveal themselves
- Energy builds for the next cycle

Rest (Month 6)

- Document and share learnings
- Regenerate creative energy
- Let insights percolate
- Prepare for the next spark

This isn't just personal development—it's future-proofing. In a world where industries transform overnight, your capacity for rapid learning becomes your most valuable asset.

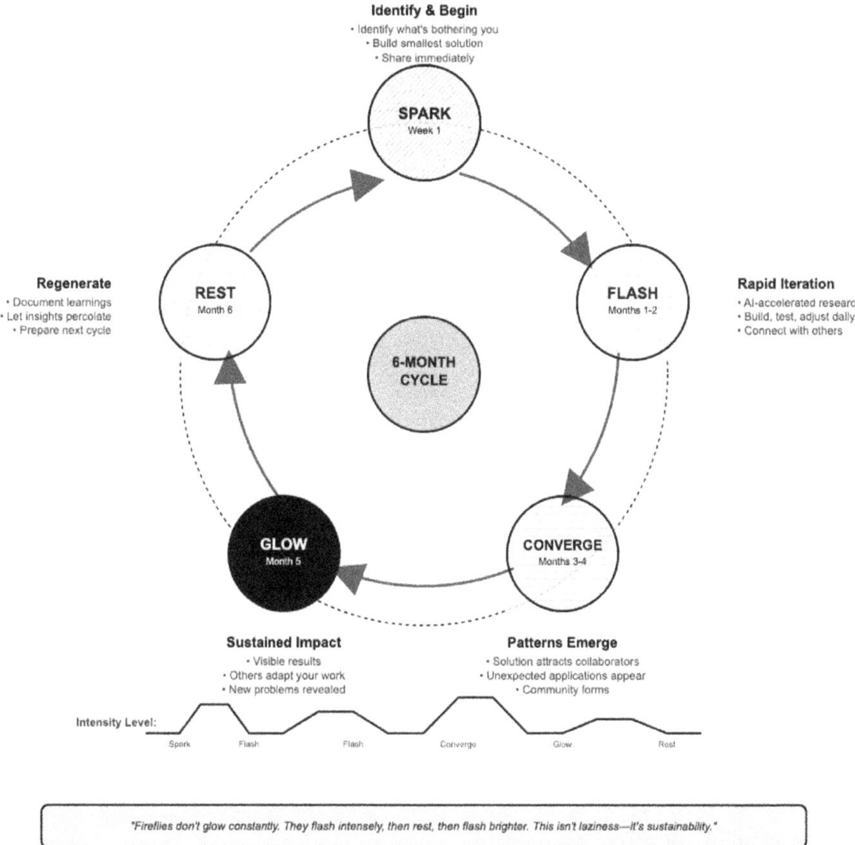
The Six-Month Firefly Sprint
From Spark to Sustained Glow
Identify & Begin
• Identify what's bothering you
• Build smallest solution
• Share immediately
SPARK
Week 1
Rapid Iteration
• AI-accelerated research
• Build, test, adjust daily
• Connect with others
FLASH
Months 1-2
6-MONTH CYCLE
CONVERGE
Months 3-4
Patterns Emerge
• Solution attracts collaborators
• Unexpected applications appear
• Community forms
GLOW
Month 5
Sustained Impact
• Visible results
• Others adapt your work
• New problems revealed
REST
Month 6
Regenerate
• Document learnings
• Let insights percolate
• Prepare next cycle
Intensity Level:
Spark
Flash
Flash
Converge
Glow
Rest
"Fireflies don't glow constantly. They flash intensely, then rest, then flash brighter. This isn't laziness—it's sustainability."

Figure 6: The Six-Month Firefly Sprint - From Spark to Sustained Glow. This cycle maps the natural rhythm of transformative learning in firefly time. Week 1 (Spark): Identify what's bothering you and build the smallest possible solution. Months 1-2 (Flash): Rapid iterations using AI-accelerated research and daily adjustments. Months 3-4 (Converge): Patterns emerge as your solution attracts collaborators and reveals unexpected applications. Month 5 (Glow): Sustained impact becomes visible as others adapt your work. Month 6 (Rest): Document learnings and regenerate creative energy. The intensity graph below shows the flash-and-rest pattern—high-energy bursts followed by integration periods. This isn't just a timeline; it's a sustainable rhythm for continuous innovation.

FROM PLANNING TO PRACTICE

The six-month cycles give you structure, but structure without curiosity is just another cage. The real magic happens when you combine disciplined learning sprints with an explorer's mindset.

Think about it: Every breakthrough in history came from someone who refused to stay in their lane. Leroy Hood was a molecular biologist who wondered what would happen if you applied computer code to genetic sequences—and invented bioinformatics, revolutionizing how we understand human health. Will Wright studied ant colonies obsessively before creating SimAnt (1991), which later influenced later releases of SimCity, using insect behavior patterns to design how virtual cities could self-organize. The teacher who explored gaming and transformed how we think about engagement.

This isn't about random wandering—it's about strategic curiosity. When you dedicate time to explore outside your expertise, you're not abandoning your core work. You're gathering fuel for innovations that your specialized colleagues will never see.

Let me show you why this matters more than ever...

USELESS UNTIL IT ISN'T

The compound effect of sustained curiosity creates careers that shouldn't exist. Corning Glass's curiosity about strengthening glass seemed pointless in 1960. There was no market need, no business case, just scientists wondering, "How strong can we make glass?" They developed Gorilla Glass and then shelved it—interesting but useless. Forty-five years later, Steve Jobs needed scratch-proof phone screens. Corning's "useless" curiosity became the foundation of every smartphone on Earth.

The lesson isn't that curiosity eventually pays off—it's that curious organizations create options for futures they can't imagine. Every sustained exploration opens doors to rooms you didn't know existed. The accountant-origami-designer and mushroom-infrastructure-engineer aren't outliers—they're what happens when curiosity compounds over time. The only question: what seemingly useless fascination will reshape your future?

THE LEARNING IMPERATIVE

The fastest way to kill your curiosity is to hoard your discoveries. Teaching forces you to:

- See your knowledge from new angles
- Expose gaps you didn't know existed
- Connect with others who push your thinking further

If you're not teaching, you're not learning deeply enough.

This follows the firefly principle of chain-reaction signaling. One flash triggers another. Your learning sparks someone else's curiosity, which illuminates new questions for you.

COMPOUNDING CURIOSITY

Here's what I've discovered: Curiosity compounds.

The more domains you explore, the more connections you make. The more connections you make, the more innovative your thinking becomes. The more innovative your thinking, the more valuable you become in any context.

I spent ten years traveling the world in a constant state of curiosity, compounding my imagination and innovative capacity. Each new environment didn't just add knowledge—it multiplied possibilities.

But curiosity requires intentional cultivation. Without the systematic practices outlined in this chapter, it withers under the pressure of daily responsibility.

FIREFLY FLASHPOINT

Reality check: Curiosity costs time, energy, and risk.
But what's the real cost of letting it die?
Look around your office. See any walking dead?

THE PLATEAU PROBLEM

Every explorer hits plateaus—moments when learning feels mechanical, when nothing sparks excitement, when you question if continued growth is worth it.

This isn't failure. It's a signal that you're ready for a different type of challenge. The plateau is where most people quit, but it's actually where real explorers are born.

When you hit a plateau:

1. Change your environment radically.
2. Seek out people who intimidate you intellectually.
3. Tackle a problem you're completely unqualified to solve.
4. Teach what you know to someone who knows nothing.

The plateau isn't an ending—it's a launching pad.

FOR THOSE WHO'VE LOST THEIR SPARK

If you're a leader or learner who feels curiosity has died, here's the uncomfortable truth: You've probably optimized yourself into a corner, becoming so good at what you do that you've stopped growing.

The cure:

1. **Become a beginner again**: Choose something where you have zero expertise. Feel the discomfort of not knowing.
2. **Break your patterns**: If you always read business books, read poetry. If you network with peers, seek out people who are twenty years younger or older than you to mentor.
3. **Create unnecessary things**: Build something that has no ROI, no strategic value, and no practical application. Remember the magic of what creation without pressure feels like: building sandcastles on the beach, drawing whatever jumped into your mind… just because.
4. **Document your ignorance**: Keep a journal of what you don't know. Celebrate questions without answers.

THE LONG GAME

We're preparing for a future that's difficult to imagine but essential to navigate.

As AI transforms every industry, spaces are becoming catalysts for societal change and ecological harmony. The cultivation of human creativity is becoming our ultimate frontier. The old order is dissolving into dynamic intergenerational communities where learning is fluid, personalized, and driven by real experience.

What happens when AI personalizes learning to every culture, devices merge with our biology, students walk through quantum classrooms, and wonder replaces worksheets?

The question isn't whether these changes will happen. It's whether you'll be an explorer who helps shape them or a bystander who gets shaped by them.

Your firefly light isn't just personal illumination—it's collective navigation. In the darkness of uncertainty, we need explorers who never stop glowing, never stop questioning, never stop building toward possibilities we can barely imagine.

THE EXPLORER'S COMMITMENT

Keeping your explorer alive isn't a luxury—it's a necessity. It's how you:

- Stay relevant in rapidly changing fields.
- Find joy in work that could become routine.
- Create value that others can't replicate.
- Build resilience against obsolescence.
- Contribute to humanity's collective intelligence.

The firefly that stops flashing doesn't just fail to attract mates—it fails to contribute its light to the swarm's magnificent display.

Keep your explorer alive. The future is counting on it.

THE REGENERATIVE MOMENT: YOUR EXPLORER'S NEXT CHAPTER

Before you close this book, before you return to the familiar, pause. This is your moment to commit to curiosity.

Three Questions to Reignite Your Explorer:

1. **Who will you teach what you've learned in this book, and what will they teach you in return?**

Learning without teaching is hoarding. Teaching without learning is stagnating. Find someone—a colleague, a child, a stranger—and share one insight from this journey. But here's the key: ask them to teach you something in return. Create a learning exchange, not a lecture. Start the chain reaction of curiosity.

2. **What would you explore if you had permission to be fascinated by anything for six months without having to justify its usefulness?** Strip away ROI. Ignore strategic value. Forget career advancement. What genuinely fascinates you? What mystery calls to you? That's your next six-month cycle. The things we explore without external justification often become our greatest contributions.

3. **What mystery in your field would you love to solve, even if it took the rest of your life?** Not what would advance your career. Not what would impress others. What puzzle would you work on purely for the joy of understanding? That's your North Star—the curiosity that will sustain you through plateaus, setbacks, and success.

Write your answers. Make them real. Share them with someone who will hold you accountable.

Here's the final firefly truth: Curiosity isn't a trait you have or don't have. It's a practice you maintain or abandon. It's a light you tend or let extinguish.

The explorer in you isn't dead. It might be dormant, waiting for permission to flash again. But as we learned in Chapter 7, the permission you're waiting for is already in your hands.

Light it up. The world needs your particular way of wondering.

A BRIEF INTERLUDE:

CONNECTING THE DOTS

"The future is not some place we are going, but one we are creating. The paths are not to be found, but made."

— John Schaar

We've traveled far together through these nine chapters, covering frameworks, stories, and tools for your firefly journey. Before we talk about what comes next, I want to take a moment to see how everything we've explored comes together and fulfills the promise on this book's cover.

HOW DO WE LEARN, LEAD, AND THRIVE IN THE AGE OF AI?

These can't just be marketing words. They're the pillars that determine whether you flourish or fade in the years ahead. So, let's take stock and see how the pieces fit together.

LEARN: OBSOLETE TO REGENERATIVE

We began with a shocking reality: Skills now expire every eighteen months.[92] The entire educational industrial complex—built for thirty-year careers—has now become obsolete. Remember the worrying numbers of teachers wanting to leave the profession? They're the canaries in the coal mine.

But here's the breakthrough insight: When traditional learning dies, something new emerges. ***Self-powered. Regenerative. Contagious.***

Chapter 3 exposed how testing kills wonder—that magical state where real learning happens. We've created a generation that—wisely, considering the predicament—chose test prep over discovery in Tokyo. However, Chapter 9 revealed the antidote: six-month learning cycles that sustain curiosity across decades of change.

The Firefly Essential Insight: In the age of AI, the ability to learn faster than your tools evolve is your only sustainable advantage. It's not what you know, but how quickly you can un-know and relearn.

LEAD: PERMISSION TO OWNERSHIP

Remember Lou Groen and his Filet-O-Fish? Sarah Blakely with her cut-up pantyhose? They didn't wait for permission. They took ownership. That's the shift that changes everything.

Chapter 6 revealed the fusion formula: ancient wisdom + modern tools = unstoppable innovation. It's like Patagonia building a billion-dollar business on environmental principles, or Finnish teachers transforming education by trusting professionals over standardized systems.

Chapter 7 delivered the wake-up call: You're addicted to permission. But the cure is simple—take ownership of one problem this week. Not someday. This week.

Chapter 8 moved us from dreaming to building. The Builder's Backpack gave you five tools that separate perpetual planners from actual creators. The 72-hour rule that forces action. The ugly baby principle that kills perfectionism.

The Game-Changing Truth: Organizations don't give permission to people who might do something someday. They provide resources to people who are already doing something valuable. The permission slip you're waiting for? You're holding it.

THRIVE: SURVIVAL TO SYNCHRONIZED BRILLIANCE

Thriving isn't about working harder—it's about sustainable brilliance. The firefly principle in action: Flash intensely, rest completely, emerge stronger.

Remember the reinvention racket from Chapter 5? Those million-dollar-plus innovation centers that changed nothing? Thriving means seeing through the performance and building what actually works. It's like Microsoft's transformation—not through consultants but by changing one hiring criterion: learn-it-alls over know-it-alls.

The compound effect from Chapter 7: Your first small act of ownership triggers confidence. Confidence enables bigger ownership. Bigger ownership attracts collaborators. Suddenly, you're not just solving problems—you're creating problem-solvers.

The Transformation Formula: Individual sparks become collective brilliance when authentic signals synchronize. You don't adapt to change; you become change.

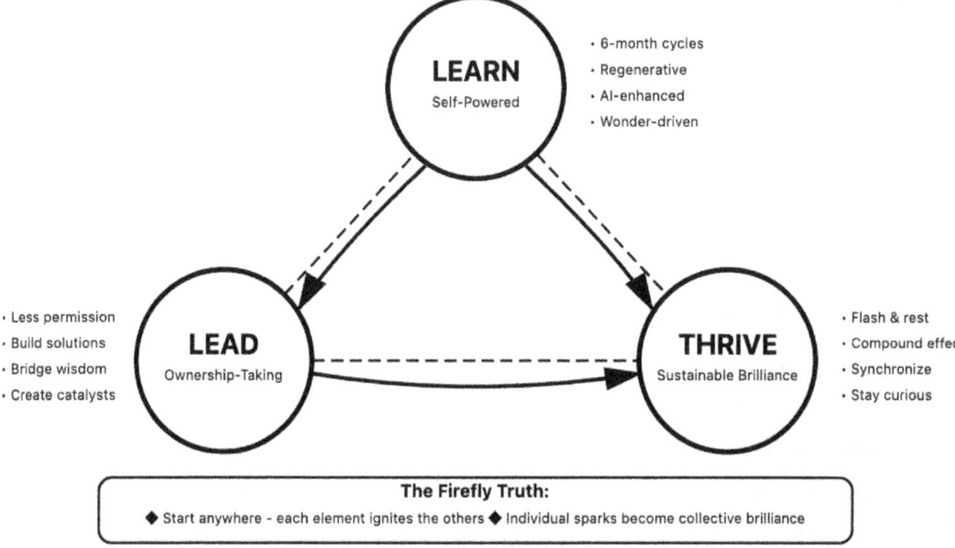
The Firefly Integration: Learn → Lead → Thrive
Not Sequential Steps, but a Simultaneous Transformation
LEARN
Self-Powered
· 6-month cycles
· Regenerative
· AI-enhanced
· Wonder-driven
LEAD
Ownership-Taking
· Less permission
· Build solutions
· Bridge wisdom
· Create catalysts
THRIVE
Sustainable Brilliance
· Flash & rest
· Compound effect
· Synchronize
· Stay curious
The Firefly Truth:
◆ Start anywhere - each element ignites the others ◆ Individual sparks become collective brilliance

Figure 7: The Firefly Integration - How Learn, Lead, and Thrive Create Sustained Transformation - This diagram illustrates the three core capabilities as an interconnected system rather than sequential steps. The arrows demonstrate how Learn (self-powered discovery) flows into both Lead (ownership-taking) and Thrive (sustainable brilliance), while Lead also enables Thrive. The dashed triangle connecting all three emphasizes that these aren't isolated skills—you can enter at any point and activate the entire system.

THE INTEGRATION REVOLUTION

Here's what separates this book from every other "future of work" manifesto: These aren't sequential steps; they're simultaneous transformations.

Watch how it works:

- The moment you start learning differently (self-powered, curiosity-driven), you naturally begin leading because others want what you have.

- The moment you lead by building real solutions, you create conditions for thriving.
- The moment you thrive sustainably, you model a new way of learning.

It's not a ladder; it's a spiral.
Each element amplifies the others.

FIREFLY MOMENTS

The evidence is overwhelming:

- Associated Press journalists freed from data processing to do actual journalism.
- Parents creating micro-schools that outperform traditional education.
- Early firefly adopters use six-month cycles to reinvent careers, while others wait for retraining.

The tools are democratizing:

- AI that turns ideas into prototypes in hours.
- Global communities forming around shared challenges.
- No-code platforms making everyone a builder.

The only scarce resource? Courage.

THE CHOICE THAT CHANGES EVERYTHING

We're preparing for a future where:

- AI handles routine thinking so that humans focus on the unprecedented.

- Hierarchies dissolve into dynamic communities.
- The ability to learn, lead, and thrive becomes the only currency that matters.

You have the framework. The Builder's Backpack. The six-month firefly plan. The evidence that ordinary people are already extraordinary builders.

Now comes the moment that separates those who read about change from those who create it.

The question isn't whether you understand firefly thinking.

The question is: What will you build first?

In the end, this book isn't about surviving the age of AI. It's about becoming the kind of human the age of AI needs—regenerative learners, ownership-taking leaders, and sustainable thrivers who light the way for others.

Your move. The world is waiting for your particular glow.

CONCLUSION

THE LIGHT CONTINUES

"The best way to predict the future is to create it."
— Peter Drucker

ONE FLASH CHANGES EVERYTHING

What a journey it's been, friends—through the collapse of old certainties and the death of wonder, through testing syndromes and reinvention rackets, through the great pretenses of our age.

But most importantly, we've discovered something profound.

In an age where artificial intelligence can process information at lightning speed, where algorithms can generate perfect answers, and where machines can simulate human responses, the most revolutionary act is to be genuinely, intermittently, beautifully human.

You've learned to see yourself not as a searchlight trying to compete with AI's computational sun, but as a firefly—carrying your own renewable source of illumination. You've discovered that brilliance isn't about being constantly on, but about knowing when to flash, when to rest, when to synchronize with others who share your commitment to authentic learning and living.

When your light feels weakest, the breakthrough is nearest.

THE DATA TELLS A STORY

A stark paradox defines our era. While AI adoption races ahead—with a recent Boston Consulting Group report finding that roughly three-quarters of organizations are using AI—human development is stalling.[93] Alarming data from sources like Gallup and the CDC show that young people's well-being is plummeting.[94] The gap between technological promise and human reality has never been wider: the same BCG study found that only 26% of companies have developed the necessary capabilities to move beyond AI pilots and generate tangible value.

What the firefly knows, and what we seem to have forgotten, is that darkness is not the absence of opportunity but the presence of it. Every gap in understanding, every moment of institutional failure, every breakdown in the old systems creates the precise conditions under which individual illumination becomes not just useful, but essential.

The firefly does not apologize for its modest brightness or wait for the sun to return—it simply glows, understanding that even the smallest light can make the difference between navigation and collision.

The darkness, in other words, is not the problem—it is the point. Your light was never meant to compete with the sun, but to shine when the sun has set.

THREE PATHS BEFORE YOU

Now you stand at a crossroads. Three paths stretch before you, and the one you choose will determine not just your future, but the future of everyone whose journey intersects with yours.

Path One: Return to the Familiar

You can close this book, appreciate the metaphors, and return to the systems that brought you here. Wait for your organization to catch up—after all, many still haven't prioritized AI on their agenda. Hope your company accelerates its pace, even though half say they need to speed up but don't know how. Trust that someone else will bridge the wisdom-innovation gap, lead the change, and sustain the wonder.

This path is safe—the safety of the graveyard. While you wait for perfect conditions, AI is eliminating entire job categories. You're not being cautious; you're committing professional suicide in slow motion. Because while you're waiting, the world is transforming at AI speed. The World Economic Forum projected that by 2025, automation could eliminate eighty-five million jobs while creating ninety-seven million new ones. The question isn't whether change is coming—it's whether you'll help shape it or be shaped by it.

Path Two: Personal Enlightenment

You can also embrace firefly thinking for yourself while waiting for others to catch up. Master prompting and pattern recognition across AI outputs while your colleagues resist. Glow privately, but be careful of feeling superior and victimized simultaneously, the curse of relentlessly complaining about the darkness around you while offering no light, transforming you into exactly the kind of person you claim to despise.

This path can feel sophisticated. You get to be the early adopter, the one who "gets it," the frustrated innovator held back by slower minds. But transformation doesn't happen through individual enlightenment. Remember the fireflies of Costa Rica? They don't achieve magnificence through one glowing brighter. They create magic when individual authenticity becomes collective synchrony. Your solo flash, no matter how brilliant, won't illuminate the forest.

> **FIELD NOTES:** Some firefly species spend up to two years underground as larvae before emerging for just a few weeks of adult life—making them nature's ultimate procrastinators who still manage to light up the world when it counts.

Path Three: Become the Catalyst

Finally, you can choose the path that scares you—where you decide the problems you see are yours to solve, where you take ownership not just of your learning, but of creating conditions where others can discover their light.

This means more than simply using AI tools. It means building complementary economies in your workplace where humans and machines work together, enhancing rather than replacing each other. It means creating learning environments that preserve wonder while embracing technology. It means being the first to flash in your organization, signaling to others: *It's safe to glow here.*

Yes, you'll face resistance. Organizations still pretending that AI isn't relevant will question your priorities. Systems invested in testing over wonder will measure your light by outdated metrics.

But this is also the path where individual sparks become collective illumination, where your courage to flash first creates permission for others to follow, where transformation actually happens.

A SWARM IS FORMING

Here's what the skeptics don't see: While institutions debate and delay, fireflies are finding each other in the darkness.

Picture this: a world where digital avatars win Nobel Prizes for groundbreaking research, where quantum learning environments let children explore the molecular structure of wonder itself, where society values giving 70% and reserving peak performance for moments that truly matter, with the rest devoted to experimental play and regenerative rest.

Are we ready for such a world? The fireflies already building it say yes.

In boardrooms worldwide, a quiet revolution is underway. A 2024 report from Deloitte found that while 77% of organizations now use or explore AI, their directors are not waiting for formal training to catch up.[95] When asked about their primary source of information on AI, their top response was self-education. They are becoming the bridges between generations—veterans sharing hard-won judgment while digital natives show how AI can scale that wisdom. This isn't replacement; it's enhancement. It's not competition; it's complementarity.

In Indian villages, farmers blend ancestral knowledge with AI-powered precision agriculture, creating food security where experts saw only scarcity. In Telangana's Khammam district, seven thousand chili farmers doubled their income using AI advisory services alongside traditional farming wisdom—yields increased 21% while pesticide use dropped 9%. Urban planners combine traditional cooling techniques with biomimetic design, proving that technology amplifies rather than erases indigenous wisdom.[96]

In schools, teachers aren't waiting for curriculum reform. At Ekya Schools in Bangalore, educators already use AI tools like ChatGPT, Midjourney, and Curipod to personalize learning while preserving what only humans can provide—the moment when understanding dawns, when confidence builds, when wonder ignites. They've proven that AI complements rather than replaces human connection, creating what they call "enriching educational experiences" across five campuses.[97] Each classroom choosing curiosity over compliance signals to others: there is another way.

In living rooms and community centers, individuals aren't waiting for institutional change. Parents form learning cooperatives, professionals create skill-sharing circles, retirees become mentors in tech hubs. Each person choosing growth over stagnation adds to the swarm: *there is another way*.

The old narrative says AI will replace us, but fireflies know better. In medicine, even in fields like radiology where AI seemed most threatening, studies show mixed results, with the combination of AI and physician expertise often outperforming either alone. Doctors aren't being replaced;

they're being augmented. In creative fields, novices with AI now perform like veterans, not by replacing experience but by accelerating the journey toward mastery. The solution isn't to compete with AI—it's to complement, using our firefly light to guide its processing power toward purposes that matter.

YOUR FUTURE SELF IS CALLING

Try something. Close your eyes for a moment.

It's five years from now. **You chose Path Three** and became a firefly catalyst.

What problem did you claim as yours? What darkness did you illuminate? What synchrony did you create?

Maybe you transformed how your organization approaches AI, not as a threat to manage but as a collaborator to embrace. You built systems where augmentation beats automation, where human creativity dances with machine efficiency.

Maybe you revolutionized learning in your community, creating spaces where children develop both deep knowledge and authentic wonder, where tests measure growth, not just retention, and where AI amplifies curiosity rather than replacing it.

Maybe you bridged generational divides in your workplace, became the translator between wisdom and innovation, helped experienced workers see AI as a tool for legacy, not obsolescence, and showed young technologists why human judgment still matters.

Or maybe you did something I can't imagine, such as solving a problem that doesn't yet have a name, building a solution that doesn't yet have a category, or creating a synchrony that doesn't yet have a pattern.

Your future self is sending you a message right now. They're telling you that every choice you make in the next six months determines whether they exist or remain just potential. They're saying: Start now. Flash first. Trust your light. ***The swarm is already forming—will you join it?***

YOUR IRREPLACEABLE CHEMISTRY

Your specific blend of experience, creativity, wisdom, and wonder is irreplaceable. No algorithm can replicate the exact chemistry of your curiosity. No model can predict the precise pattern of your insights. No artificial light can substitute for your authentic glow.

Consider this: in a recent global report from the learning platform Degreed, nearly 40% of leaders said that hard skills now have a shelf life of under two years. The same report found that 78% of leaders believe today's hard skills will be obsolete in under five years.[98] The solution, however, isn't to chase every new skill—it's to develop the uniquely human capabilities that make you adaptable to any change.

FROM OBSERVER TO CATALYST

Let me leave you with the questions that separate firefly catalysts from passive observers:

What problem in your sphere of influence are you uniquely positioned to illuminate? Not someday. Not when conditions are perfect. Now. With the resources you have. In the darkness you face.

Who is waiting for your flash to remind them of their own light? Your team, wondering if AI means obsolescence? Your children, navigating a world where answers are instant but wisdom is scarce? Your community, seeking bridges between old and new?

What would you build if you believed in the firefly principle? Those small, authentic, synchronized actions transform landscapes. Not grand plans. Not perfect strategies. Simple first flashes that signal possibility.

How will you balance the three tensions of our age?

- **Speed vs. Depth:** Can you flash quickly while glowing authentically?

- **Individual vs. Collective:** Can you maintain your unique pattern while synchronizing with others?
- **Human vs. Artificial:** Can you use AI to amplify rather than replace what makes you irreplaceable?

What's the cost of not acting? While you wait for permission, how many potential fireflies dim? While you perfect your plans, how many opportunities to synchronize pass? While you debate whether to glow, how much darker does your corner of the world become?

These questions don't need perfect answers. They need imperfect action. Fireflies don't wait for ideal conditions. They trust their inner chemistry and flash.

THE MEADOW AT MIDNIGHT

Let me take you somewhere.

It's midnight in a meadow. Maybe tonight. Maybe a decade from now, when AI has transformed everything we think we know.

The darkness feels complete. At first, nothing. Your eyes, accustomed to artificial lights, to constant screens, to endless illumination, struggle with natural darkness. The temptation rises: reach for your phone, ask AI for guidance, fill the uncertainty with artificial brightness.

But wait. Breathe. Remember what you learned about fireflies, darkness, and the beauty of intermittent light.

Then—a single flash. Brief, tentative, almost questioning: *Is anyone else out there?*

Another flash answers. Then another. Within minutes, the entire meadow pulses. Not in perfect unison—that would be artificial—but in organic synchrony. Each firefly maintains its unique pattern while contributing to something magnificent.

This is your meadow.

Currently, millions of people are reading books like this, attending workshops, and engaging in late-night conversations about what this new world means for their work, families, and futures. Each one is a potential firefly, carrying their own mixture of fear and hope, wisdom and wonder, waiting for a signal that it's safe to glow.

You could wait for someone else to flash first. You could analyze the darkness, measure the risk, and perfect your glow pattern. You could convince yourself your light is too small, too imperfect, too human to matter in this artificial age.

Or you could trust what fireflies have known for millions of years.

THE CHOICE IS NOW

The darkness isn't the enemy—it's the opportunity. Without night, there would be no need for bioluminescence. Without disruption, there would be no evolution of light.

The AI age hasn't made you obsolete; it's made you essential. And it's done this not despite your human limitations, but because of them. You are able to wonder, while AI can only process. You possess the capacity to care, while algorithms can only calculate. You have the power to create meaning, whereas machines can only identify patterns.

Old systems are dimming; some might argue they are clinging to their deathbed. Young people will potentially find themselves in a digital wilderness, with human development reaching an evolutionary stasis while technology continues to advance. The gap between AI's promise and reality continues to widen each day.

The tragedy might not be that we expected too much from our machines, but that we expected so little from ourselves.

But like fireflies emerging at dusk, small rebellions of competence are beginning to illuminate the darkness. In boardrooms where directors self-educate because waiting for formal training takes too long. In suburban neighborhoods, parents create learning cooperatives because schools can't adapt fast enough. In offices and factories, they have grown tired of waiting for the managerial class to craft the perfect policy; workers now build human-AI partnerships emerging through the simple expedient of necessity meeting opportunity.

The swarm is forming—not through central planning or institutional mandates, but through individual courage becoming collective action, through authentic flashes that create permission for others to shine, and through small lights synchronizing into transformative illumination.

Your light was never meant to shine alone, but it was always meant to shine—not just because you are uniquely gifted but because you are uniquely you, and the world has a shortage of that particular commodity.

The question isn't whether you're bright enough, ready enough, or expert enough. The question is whether you'll trust your inner chemistry and flash.

Because here's what the permission-seekers never grasp: Authenticity is not a qualification you earn but a risk you take, and the swarm is waiting not for your perfection but for your participation.

YOUR FIREFLY LEGACY

Imagine that it's decades from now. The history of the AI age is being written. What will historians say about this moment? What will they make of us? What verdict will they reach on the choices made by otherwise intelligent people who found themselves at the threshold of the AI age?

Will they write about the majority, who waited for perfect conditions that never came? Who polished their fears while opportunities passed? Who chose familiar darkness over uncertain light?

Or will they tell stories of the firefly catalysts? The ones who flashed first in their organizations. Who built bridges between wisdom and innovation? Who created learning environments where wonder survived and thrived? Who proved that in an age of artificial intelligence, authentic humanity has become our greatest asset?

The historians will have to choose between writing about those who waited for permission and those who granted it to themselves. I suspect I know which story will prove more compelling to readers who have inherited the world these choices created.

Your grandchildren won't ask if you had the perfect plan. They'll ask if you had the courage to act. They won't care if your light was the brightest. They'll care that you chose to glow.

YOUR FIRST FLASH

Here's my final challenge: **Within forty-eight hours of reading this, take one or more of these concrete actions.** Not a plan. Not a preparation. An action.

- **Document your spark:** Start capturing moments when curiosity strikes or ideas emerge.
- **Form your firefly circle**: Begin that six-month learning cycle with two or three colleagues.
- **Build your first prototype**: Create something tangible that scratches an itch you've been ignoring.
- **Start the AI conversation**: Schedule a discussion about what artificial intelligence means for your work and community.
- **Propose regenerative spaces**: Write up your vision for learning environments that sustain rather than drain energy.
- **Become a bridge**: Offer to mentor someone navigating technological transformation.

Make it small. Make it imperfect. But make it real.

The moment you flash, something magical happens. Others see your light and remember their own. Your courage grants permission. Your action creates possibility.

And suddenly, you're not alone in the darkness anymore.

THE FINAL TRUTH

The old lights are dimming. That's not a tragedy—it's an opportunity. Every ending creates space for new beginnings. Every darkness calls forth new light.

You were built for this moment. Not despite your humanity, but because of it. Not in competition with AI, but in partnership with it. Not as a solo searchlight, but as part of a magnificent swarm.

The meadow is dark. The world is waiting. Your unique light has never been more needed.

Stop waiting. Start owning.

Flash.

The darkness needs your light. Your swarm needs your signal. The future needs your specific, irreplaceable, beautifully human glow.

What are you waiting for?

Flash.

Flash.

Flash.

Your firefly-inspired journey begins now.

If this book lit something within you, pass it on. Share your flash. Tag your story with #FireflyEffect. Find your swarm at https://www.thefireflyeffectbook.com

Remember, every transformation starts with one person brave enough to glow.

GLOSSARY

CORE FIREFLY CONCEPTS

Firefly Effect – The phenomenon where individual acts of authentic, self-generated brilliance create cascading illumination across communities, transforming darkness into opportunity through synchronized yet autonomous action.

Firefly Mindset – A way of thinking that emphasizes self-powered learning, regenerative cycles, chain-reaction signaling, and organic synchronization rather than hierarchical control.

Firefly Time – Short, intensive bursts of innovation (typically six-month cycles) that create more value than decades of steady progress. Contrasts with traditional long-term planning cycles.

Firefly Thinking – The practice of generating your own light (ideas, solutions, learning) rather than waiting for external illumination or permission.

Firefly Wheel – *A six-element regenerative learning system: Dusk (foundation) → Dance (build) → Beacon (share) → Constellation (imagine) → Harmony (evaluate) → Dawn (rest) → repeat.*

EDUCATIONAL & ORGANIZATIONAL TERMS

Broken Glow – The failing light of traditional systems (education, corporate, leadership) that no longer serve their intended purpose in our rapidly changing world.

Chain Reaction Signaling – When one person's authentic learning or innovation naturally triggers similar responses in others, creating organic spread without formal mandates.

Compound Illumination – The exponential effect when multiple small acts of learning or innovation connect to create larger patterns of transformation.

Kayfabe – Originally from professional wrestling, the elaborate performance where everyone knows something is staged but plays along anyway. Used to describe institutional theater.

Performance Theater – Organizational activities that simulate progress without creating actual change (e.g., innovation labs that produce no innovations).

Regenerative Cycles – The natural rhythm of intense activity followed by rest and integration, like fireflies that flash and rest rather than glowing continuously.

Reinvention Racket – The systematic waste of resources on fake transformation initiatives that use buzzwords and theater instead of creating real change.

Testing Syndrome – The educational obsession with standardized measurement that kills wonder, curiosity, and authentic learning.

LEARNING & DEVELOPMENT TERMS

Builder's Backpack – Five essential tools for taking ownership: 1) Bravery anchored in principle, 2) Prototype thinking, 3) Scientific obsession, 4) Emotional resilience, 5) Strategic humor.

Dirty Prototyping – Creating rough, imperfect versions of ideas quickly to test and learn, rather than waiting for perfect conditions.

Integration Week – Periods with no scheduled activities, allowing time to process, reflect, and create deeper understanding.

Ownership Levels – Three stages of taking responsibility: Personal (your own growth), Project (solving specific problems), and Systems (transforming environments).

Permission Addiction – The learned helplessness of waiting for external approval before taking action or making changes.

Six-Month Sprint – A focused learning or building cycle aligned with firefly time, allowing for rapid iteration and adaptation.

CULTURAL & WISDOM TERMS

Ikigai – Japanese concept meaning "reason for being" or putting your soul into your work.

Kaizen – Japanese philosophy of continuous improvement through small, incremental changes.

Satya – Sanskrit term meaning "truth" or living authentically.

Ubuntu – African philosophy meaning "I am because we are," emphasizing collective humanity and interdependence.

VUCA – Acronym for Volatile, Uncertain, Complex, and Ambiguous—describing our current world conditions.

TECHNOLOGY & INNOVATION TERMS

AI Washing – The practice of labeling existing systems as "AI-powered" without meaningful integration or improvement.

Complementarity Economy – A workplace where humans and AI enhance each other rather than compete, with each focusing on their unique strengths.

Digital Transformation Theater – Expensive technological initiatives that change tools but not underlying behaviors or outcomes.

Horizon Scanning – The practice of identifying weak signals of future change and acting on them before they become mainstream.

No-Code Platforms – Tools that allow anyone to build applications and solutions without programming knowledge.

METAPHORICAL TERMS

False Glow – Inauthentic light that attracts but ultimately consumes, like certain firefly species that mimic others' patterns to prey on them. Represents fake innovation or harmful systems.

Flickering Bulbs – People or systems running on external power that fails intermittently, contrasting with self-powered firefly light.

Living Constellation – A dynamic community where individual lights create collective patterns of beauty and meaning.

Signals from the Future – Warning messages that show what happens when we fail to adapt, presented as diary entries from a possible future.

Swarm Intelligence – The collective wisdom that emerges when individual fireflies synchronize their patterns without central control.

KEY PHRASES

"Flash or Fade" – The choice between taking action (flashing your light) or becoming irrelevant (fading into darkness).

"Growth Equals Glow" – The principle that authentic development manifests as visible positive change.

"Performance Over Progress" – The tendency of institutions to prioritize the appearance of innovation over actual transformation.

"Racing Toward the Divide" – The growing gap between organizations embracing AI and those resisting change.

"The Great Pretend" – The collective act of maintaining systems everyone knows are broken while pretending they work.

THANK YOU FOR READING MY BOOK!

DOWNLOAD YOUR FREE GIFTS

Just to say thanks for buying and reading my book,
I would like to give you a few free bonus gifts, no strings attached!

To Download Now, Visit:

I appreciate your interest in my book and value your feedback as it helps me improve future versions of this book. I would appreciate it if you could leave your invaluable review on Amazon.com with your feedback.

Thank you!

ENDNOTES

[1] Phuong Pham and Jingtao Wang, "AttentiveLearner: Improving Mobile MOOC Learning via Implicit Heart Rate Tracking," in *International Conference on Artificial Intelligence in Education* (New York: Springer, 2015), 367-376.

[2] OpenAI Unhobbles O1, Epitomizing the Relentless Pace of AI Progress: Center for AI Policy: CAIP," Center for AI Policy, accessed July 11, 2025, https://www.centeraipolicy.org/work/openai-unhobbles-o1-epitomizing-the-relentless-pace-of-ai-progress.

[3] Frank Arute et al., "Quantum Supremacy Using a Programmable Superconducting Processor," *Nature* 574, no. 7779 (2019): 505-510.

[4] "Tech Layoff Tracker and Doge Layoff Tracker," Layoffs.fyi, February 25, 2025, https://layoffs.fyi/.

[5] Clare Duffy and Catherine Thorbecke, "Microsoft to Lay Off 10,000 Employees," *CNN Business*, January 18, 2023, https://www.cnn.com/2023/01/18/tech/microsoft-layoffs/index.html.

[6] Benjamin Mullin and Katie Robertson, "BuzzFeed News Is Shutting Down," *The New York Times*, April 20, 2023.

[7] "BuzzFeed, Inc.. Completes Strategic and Organizational Changes Following a Transformative 2024." Global Press Release & Newswire Distribution Services, March 13, 2025. https://www.businesswire.com/news/home/20250313679528/en/BuzzFeed-Inc.-Completes-Strategic-and-Organizational-Changes-Following-a-Transformative-2024

[8] World Economic Forum, "The Future of Jobs Report 2020," October 2020, https://www.weforum.org/reports/the-future-of-jobs-report-2020/.

[9] Eric Hazan et al., "The Economic Potential of Generative AI: The Next Productivity Frontier," McKinsey Global Institute, June 14, 2023, https://www.mckinsey.com/mgi/our-research/the-economic-potential-of-generative-ai-the-next-productivity-frontier

[10] Institute for the Future. The Next Era of Human-Machine Partnerships: Emerging Technologies' Impact on Society & Work in 2030. Commissioned by Dell Technologies, 2017. https://www.delltechnologies.com/content/dam/delltechnologies/assets/perspectives/2030/pdf/SR1940_IFTFforDellTechnologies_Human-Machine_070517_readerhigh-res.pdf

[11]World Economic Forum, "The Future of Jobs Report 2023," May 2023, https://www.weforum.org/reports/the-future-of-jobs-report-2023/.

[12] Patrick Noack, personal communication, Dubai AI Retreat 2025, Dubai Future Foundation, Dubai.

[13] Andy Clark, *Natural-Born Cyborgs: Minds, Technologies, and the Future of Human Intelligence* (Oxford: Oxford University Press, 2003).

[14] E. Guzik et al., "The Creative Potential of ChatGPT: Testing GPT-4 on the Torrance Tests of Creative Thinking" (paper presented at the Southern Oregon University Creativity Conference, University of Montana, May 2023).

[15] J. King, "Alpha School Uses AI to Teach Students Academics for Just Two Hours a Day," *FOX 7 Austin*, September 23, 2024, https://www.fox7austin.com/news/alpha-school-two-hour-learning-ai-tutor-austin-texas.

[16] Laura Meckler, Prayag Gordy, and Clara Ence Morse, "Homeschooling Soared during the Pandemic. Now It's the Fastest-Growing Form of Education," *The Washington Post*, May 30, 2023, https://www.washingtonpost.com/education/interactive/2023/homeschooling-growth-data-by-district/.

[17] Dawn McCarty and Beth Jinks, "Kodak Files for Bankruptcy as Digital Era Spells End to Film," Bloomberg, January 19, 2012, https://www.bloomberg.com/news/articles/2012-01-19/kodak-photography-pioneer-files-for-bankruptcy-protection-1-.

[18] 2023 Training Industry Report," *Training Magazine*, November/December 2023.

[19] LinkedIn Learning, "Workplace Learning Report 2023" (LinkedIn, 2023).

[20] Michael Beer, Magnus Finnström, and Derek Schrader, "The Great Training Robbery," Harvard Business School Working Paper 16-121 (2016).

[21] Alan M. Saks and Monica Belcourt, "An Investigation of Training Activities and Transfer of Training in Organizations," Human Resource Management 45, no. 4 (2006): 629-648.

[22] Hiroko Oyamada, *The Factory*, translated by David Boyd (New York: New Directions Publishing Corporation, 2019).

[23] "WeWork's Rise and Fall: From $47 Billion Valuation to Bankruptcy: Company Business News." mint, November 8, 2023. https://www.livemint.com/companies/news/weworks-rise-and-fall-from-47-billion-valuation-to-bankruptcy-11699404736798.html.

[24] Takaharu Tezuka, "The Best Kindergarten You've Ever Seen," TED Talk, September 2014, https://www.ted.com/talks/takaharu_tezuka_the_best_kindergarten_you_ve_ever_seen

[25] "Why the Inventor of the Cubicle Came to Despise His Own Creation." History.com, May 28, 2025. https://www.history.com/articles/why-the-inventor-of-the-cubicle-came-to-despise-his-own-creation.

[26] Michelle Chouinard, "Children's Questions: A Mechanism for Cognitive Development," Monographs of the Society for Research in Child Development 72, no. 1 (2007): 1-129.

[27] Susan Engel, *The Hungry Mind: The Origins of Curiosity in Childhood* (Cambridge, MA: Harvard University Press, 2015).

[28] Peter Cappelli and Anna Tavis, "The Performance Management Revolution," *Harvard Business Review*, October 2016.

[29] Jaak Panksepp, *Affective Neuroscience: The Foundations of Human and Animal Emotions* (New York: Oxford University Press, 1998).

[30] Ken Robinson, "Do Schools Kill Creativity?" TED, 2006, https://www.ted.com/talks/sir_ken_robinson_do_schools_kill_creativity?language=en.

[31] Friedman, Thomas L. "How to Get a Job at Google." The New York Times, February 22, 2014.

[32] Gartner, Inc. "Gartner HR Research Finds the High Cost of Ineffective Training Can Amount to $13.5M Annually for a 1,000-Employee Organization." Press Release, October 11, 2018.

[33] Laszlo Bock, *Work Rules!: Insights from Inside Google That Will Transform How You Live and Lead* (New York: Twelve, 2015).

[34] Alec Ash, "Is China's Gaokao the World's Toughest School Exam?" *The Guardian*, October 12, 2016, https://www.theguardian.com/world/2016/oct/12/gaokao-china-toughest-school-exam-in-world.

[35] AvianWe. "Atal Tinkering Labs." Atal Innovation Mission (AIM). Accessed July 11, 2025. https://aim.gov.in/atl.php.

[36] "Human Flourishing Curriculum." Hakuba International School. Accessed July 11, 2025. https://www.hakuba-is.jp/human-flourishing-curriculum.

[37] "Our Journey." Dalton School Hong Kong. Accessed July 11, 2025. https://dshk.edu.hk/our-journey/.

[38] Laszlo Bock, *Work Rules!: Insights from Inside Google That Will Transform How You Live and Lead* (New York: Twelve, 2015).

[39] Sugata Mitra, "The Child-Driven Education," TED Talk, July 2010.

[40] Tom Peters and Robert H. Waterman Jr., *In Search of Excellence* (New York: Harper & Row, 1982).

[41] Lee, Angie. "Māori Speech AI Model Helps Preserve and Promote New Zealand Indigenous Language." NVIDIA Blog, November 5, 2024. https://blogs.nvidia.com/blog/te-hiku-media-maori-speech-ai/.

[42] E. Guzik, C. Gilde, and C. Byrge, "The Creative Potential of ChatGPT: Testing GPT-4 on the Torrance Tests of Creative Thinking" (paper presented at the Southern Oregon University Creativity Conference, University of Montana, May 2023).

[43] "Reimagining the Shopping Cart," IDEO, accessed July 11, 2025, https://www.ideo.com/journal/reimagining-the-shopping-cart.

[44] United Nations Development Programme, Human Development Report 2025: *A Matter of Choice: People and Possibilities in the Age of Artificial Intelligence (AI)* (UNDP, 2025).

[45] Ethan Mollick, *Co-Intelligence: Living and Working with AI* (New York: Portfolio, 2024).

[46] DinarStandard, *Bangladesh 2050: Towards Socio-Economic Prosperity* (Insights Brief) (Dhaka, Bangladesh: DinarStandard, June 2025).

[47] Smith, Scott, and Madeline Ashby. *How to Future: Leading and Sense-making in an Age of Hyperchange.* London: Kogan Page, 2020.

[48] Healthcare Dive. "STAT: IBM's Watson Gave 'Unsafe and Incorrect' Cancer Treatment Advice." Healthcare Dive, July 26, 2018. https://www.healthcaredive.com/news/stat-ibms-watson-gave-unsafe-and-incorrect-cancer-treatment-advice/528666/.

[49] Howard Blume, "L.A. School District Demands Refund from Apple over iPad Curriculum Problems," *Los Angeles Times,* April 16, 2015.

[50] Gina Keating, *Netflixed: The Epic Battle for America's Eyeballs* (New York: Portfolio/Penguin, 2012).

[51] Thomas Gryta and Ted Mann, "GE Powered the American Century—Then It Burned Out," *The Wall Street Journal*, December 13, 2018.

[52] Natasha Singer, "IBM Pulls Back on Watson AI for Drug Discovery and Education," *The New York Times*, July 27, 2020.

[53] Jacquie McNish and Sean Silcoff, *Losing the Signal: The Untold Story Behind the Extraordinary Rise and Spectacular Fall of BlackBerry* (New York: Flatiron Books, 2015).

[54] Carol S. Dweck, *Mindset: The Psychology of Success* (New York: Random House, 2006).

[55] Russell Cailey. "Beyond Classrooms," video, TEDxDKU, 2023. https://www.youtube.com/watch?v=jvSLKC7McAc

[56] M. A. Brackett, *Permission to Feel: Unlocking the Power of Emotions to Help Our Kids, Ourselves, and Our Society Thrive* (New York: Celadon Books, 2019).

[57] "HSBC 'Different Points of Value,'" *The Financial Brand*, July 28, 2022, https://thefinancialbrand.com/news/bank-marketing/hsbc-brand-6361.

[58] Leigh Gallagher, *The Airbnb Story* (Boston: Houghton Mifflin Harcourt, 2017).

[59] Allan Lee, "When Empowering Employees Works and When It Doesn't," *Harvard Business Review*, March 2, 2018.

[60] Papa Reo. accessed July 23, 2025, https://papareo.nz/.

[61] Associated Press, "AP to Automate Quarterly Earnings Stories," *AP News*, July 1, 2014.

[62] U.S. Food & Drug Administration, "Artificial Intelligence and Machine Learning (AI/ML)-Enabled Medical Devices," FDA.gov, July 30, 2023, https://www.fda.gov/medical-devices/software-medical-device-samd/artificial-intelligence-and-machine-learning-aiml-enabled-medical-devices.

[63] Hannah Murphy, "FDA Has Approved over 1,000 Clinical AI Applications, with Most Aimed at Radiology," *Health Imaging*, January 13, 2025, https://healthimaging.com/topics/artificial-intelligence/fda-has-approved-over-1000-clinical-ai-applications-most-aimed-radiology.

[64] Martin E. P. Seligman, *Helplessness: On Depression, Development, and Death* (New York: W. H. Freeman, 1975).

[65] Julian B. Rotter, "Generalized Expectancies for Internal Versus External Control of Reinforcement," *Psychological Monographs: General and Applied 80, no. 1* (1966): 1-28.

[66] Robert Half, "Empowering Employees: New Research Reveals Why Managers Must Foster 'Intrapreneurship,'" press release, July 10, 2018, https://press.roberthalf.com/news_releases?l=50&o=650

[67] Clayton Christensen, *The Innovator's Dilemma* (Boston: Harvard Business Review Press, 1997).

[68] Microsoft, "Work Trend Index Annual Report: Will AI Fix Work?" March 9, 2023, https://www.microsoft.com/en-us/worklab/work-trend-index/will-ai-fix-work.

[69] Gartner, Inc., "Gartner HR Research Reveals Only 31% of Organizations Believe They Have the Culture to Succeed with Hybrid Work," press release, February 14, 2023, https://www.gartner.com/en/newsroom/press-releases/2018-09-20-gartner-says-only-31-percent-of-hr-leaders-believe-their-organizations-have-the-culture-necessary-to-drive-performance

[70] Ray Kroc and Robert Anderson, *Grinding It Out: The Making of McDonald's* (Chicago: Contemporary Books, 1977).

[71] Howard Schultz and Dori Jones Yang, *Pour Your Heart Into It: How Starbucks Built a Company One Cup at a Time* (New York: Hyperion, 1997).

[72] Reiji Asakura, *Revolutionaries at Sony: The Making of the Sony PlayStation* (New York: McGraw-Hill, 2000).

[73] Amy Webb, *The Signals Are Talking: Why Today's Fringe Is Tomorrow's Mainstream* (New York: PublicAffairs, 2016).

[74] William Gibson, interview by Terry Gross, *Fresh Air*, NPR, August 31, 1999.

[75] Alpha School, "Annual Learning Outcomes Report," 2023, https://alphaschool.com/outcomes.

[76] Scott Smith and Madeline Ashby, *How to Future: Leading and Sense-making in an Age of Hyperchange* (London: Kogan Page, 2020).

[77] Peter Schwartz, *The Art of the Long View: Planning for the Future in an Uncertain World* (New York: Currency Doubleday, 1991).

[78] Jamais Cascio, *Phase Transition: The Next Decade of Futures* (Palo Alto, CA: Institute for the Future, 2020).

[79] Jane McGonigal, *Imaginable: How to See the Future Coming and Feel Ready for Anything* (New York: Spiegel & Grau, 2022).

[80] Ron Finley, "A Guerrilla Gardener in South Central LA," TED Conferences, February 2013, https://www.ted.com/talks/ron_finley_a_guerrilla_gardener_in_south_central_la.

[81] C. Coyle, "Ron Finley: Urban Gangsta Gardener," *Los Angeles Times*, May 15, 2016.

[82] Howard Schultz and Joanne Gordon, *Onward: How Starbucks Fought for Its Life without Losing Its Soul* (Emmaus, PA: Rodale Books, 2011).

[83] Starbucks Corporation, *2020 Annual Report* (Seattle: Starbucks Corporation, 2020).

[84] Ray Dalio, *Principles: Life and Work* (New York: Simon & Schuster, 2017).

[85] Isaacson, Walter. *Elon Musk*. New York: Simon & Schuster, 2023.

[86] Isaacson, Walter. *Steve Jobs*. Simon & Schuster, 2011.

[87] Ben Mezrich, *The Accidental Billionaires* (New York: Doubleday, 2009).

[88] TechCrunch, "How Dropbox Started," presentation, 2013.

[89] Salman Khan, *The One World Schoolhouse: Education Reimagined* (New York: Twelve, 2012).

[90] Tara Brach, *Radical Acceptance: Embracing Your Life with the Heart of a Buddh*a (New York: Bantam, 2003).

[91] Walmart, "Live Better U Education Program," 2024, https://corporate.walmart.com/about/working-at-walmart/live-better-u.

[92] World Economic Forum, "Future of Jobs Report 2023," 2023

[93] Boston Consulting Group, "BCG AI Radar: The CEO's Guide to the Generative AI Revolution," November 29, 2023.

[94] Gallup, "State of the Global Workplace: 2023 Report," June 13, 2023.

[95] Stephen Garrido et al., "AI and the Board: A New Era of Governance," Deloitte and Ivey Business School, 2024.

[96] "Farmers in India Are Using AI for Agriculture – Here's How They Could Inspire the World," World Economic Forum, accessed July 8, 2025, https://www.weforum.org/stories/2024/01/how-indias-ai-agriculture-boom-could-inspire-the-world/

[97] Ekya Schools, "Chatgpt and beyond: How to Handle AI in Schools," Ekya Schools, March 29, 2025, https://ekyaschools.com/blog/chatgpt-and-beyond-how-to-handle-ai-in-schools/.

[98] Degreed, "State of Skills 2024: The Skills-First Organization," 2024, https://get.degreed.com/state-of-skills-report

www.ingramcontent.com/pod-product-compliance
Lightning Source LLC
Chambersburg PA
CBHW031403180326
41458CB00043B/6597/J

* 9 7 8 1 9 6 8 2 5 0 6 6 9 *